IMAGES ACROSS THE AGES

ITALIAN PORTRAITS

Dorothy
and
Thomas Hoobler

RSVP
**RAINTREE
STECK-VAUGHN**
P U B L I S H E R S
The Steck-Vaughn Company

Austin, Texas

Cover and interior design: Suzanne Beck
Illustrations: Kim Fujiwara
Electronic Production: Scott Melcer
Project Manager: Joyce Spicer

Library of Congress Cataloging-in-Publication Data

Hoobler, Dorothy.
    Italian portraits / by Dorothy and Thomas Hoobler : illustrated by Kim Fujiwara.
        p.   cm. — (Images across the ages)
    Includes bibliographical references and index.
    Summary: Presents biographical sketches of such prominent Italians as Julius Caesar, St. Francis of Assisi, Michelangelo, Galileo, Suetonius, and Maria Montessori.
    ISBN 0-8114-6377-X
    1. Italian — Biography — Juvenile literature.   [1. Italy — Biography.]
I. Hoobler, Thomas. II. Fujiwara, Kim, ill. III. Title. IV. Series: Hoobler, Dorothy. Images across the ages.
CT1124.H67   1993
920.045—dc20   92-13641
                                                      CIP AC

Printed and bound in the United States by Lake Book, Melrose Park, IL
1 2 3 4 5 6 7 8 9 0 LB 98 97 96 95 94 93

CONTENTS

INTRODUCTION

THE CITY THAT CONQUERED THE WORLD

"I sing of arms and the man...." With these words Rome's greatest poet, Virgil, began *The Aeneid*, an epic tale of war and heroes. "The man" was Aeneas, a Trojan chieftain who fought bravely against the Greeks in the Trojan War. After the Greeks tricked their way into Troy inside a hollow horse, they slaughtered the inhabitants: "Everywhere sorrow, everywhere panic, everywhere the image of death."

As flames engulfed Troy, Aeneas and his family escaped. Aeneas carried his son in his arms and his old father on his shoulders. Aeneas' mother, Venus, the goddess of love, guided them to safety.

After many adventures, Aeneas arrived at the shores of Italy and sailed up the Tiber River to the kingdom of Latium. Aeneas won the hand of the king's daughter, and their descendants ruled Latium.

Many generations later twin boys, Romulus and Remus, were born in Latium. Their birth caused a scandal, for their mother was a Vestal Virgin, one of the guardians of the city's sacred fire, women who were pledged to chastity. She told her uncle, who had seized the throne from her father, that she had been raped by Mars, the god of war. The cruel king ordered the infants drowned in the Tiber River.

According to legend, the twins were placed in a basket and floated onto the water. By good luck, the basket came to rest on dry land near a fig tree. A she-wolf suckled the babies while a woodpecker dropped food from the tree. A shepherd found the infants and took them home. He and his wife raised the twins, who grew up sturdy and boisterous. When Remus was a teenager, he was captured in a fight with the king's soldiers. Romulus hurried to rescue his brother and killed the king. They then restored their grandfather to his throne.

Romulus and Remus wanted to found a city of their own. To do so, they returned to the hilly area where they had been nurtured by the she-wolf. Soon the twins quarreled about which one would be king. In ancient Italy people called *augurs* interpreted the flight of birds to reach decisions. So the brothers went to separate hills to watch for a sign as to who should rule.

Remus sped to the Aventine Hill, and soon six vultures soared above him. He claimed victory. But then twelve vultures appeared above the Palatine Hill where Romulus waited. Romulus was declared the winner and became the ruler of the city, which was named Rome after him.

By tradition, the date of the city's founding was 753 B.C. Romulus built his city on the Palatine Hill. He raised walls to guard the new settlement. One day Remus leaped over the wall to taunt his twin. Romulus killed his brother and exclaimed: "So perish any other who leaps over my walls." It was a boast that few would challenge in the years that followed, for Rome took on the warlike quality of Romulus. Over time it absorbed the six other hills in the area to gain the name "the city of the seven hills."

A series of kings ruled after Romulus. In 509 B.C. the last king, a cruel and vicious ruler, was overthrown. Rome became a republic. In place of the king were two consuls who ruled jointly for a term of one year. Either of the consuls could cancel the decisions of the other. A Senate, made up of the most influential and highborn Romans, advised the consuls. A more democratic Assembly proposed and passed laws.

The republic spread beyond the hills and over time conquered all of today's Italy. As the Romans expanded their domain, they came into contact with other cultures. The Etruscans, who lived to the north in a region now called Tuscany, set a permanent stamp on Roman culture.

They taught Romans how to tend grape vines for wine-making and to grow olive trees for their fruit and oil. The Etruscans were first-rate engineers, and from them the Romans learned how to construct strong and permanent roads. The Romans also adopted the traditions of Etruscan art, some of their religious beliefs, and their love for gladiatorial combat. The Romans, who had not developed any means of writing, also adopted the Etruscan alphabet.

Around the time Romulus was founding Rome, Greece established colonies in the southern part of the Italian peninsula. These settlements brought to Italy the glories of Greek art, philosophy, and drama. The Romans found Greek culture so impressive that they adopted much of it for their own.

Rome's hard-fighting legions spread the city's power and culture beyond Italy. At its height in the second century A.D., the Roman Empire controlled all the lands surrounding the Mediterranean Sea. They included northern Africa, western Asia, and parts of Europe beyond the Alps.

Even today, Roman buildings, statues, and roads still exist as reminders of that mighty empire, but it had a more lasting influence—in culture, law, and language. The Latin language formed the basis of the Romance languages— Spanish, French, Portuguese, Italian, and Rumanian. Anyone who studies Latin will see how many English words come from it as well. The culture of Rome, blending the best of the ancient world with the considerable achievements of the Romans themselves, forms the basis of what we know as western civilization.

After the fall of Rome in A.D. 492, the peninsula of Italy was divided into smaller states until the nineteenth century. Italians, nevertheless, continued their amazing record of contributions to civilization. The city of Rome became home to the pope, the spiritual leader of one of the world's great religions—Roman Catholicism. Italian geniuses in painting, sculpture, music, architecture, and science have enriched the world. The Italian biographical portraits in this short book provide only a glimpse of some of the most interesting and brilliant people in history.

"I Came, I Saw, I Conquered"— Julius Caesar

Though he was a prisoner on a pirate ship, Gaius Julius Caesar remained his usual cool and confident self. The pirates had captured the young Roman on his way to Rhodes, where he intended to study public speaking with a Greek master. Caesar was a very proud young man, part of an ancient family. When the pirates demanded a ransom of twenty talents, he scoffed and claimed he was worth fifty. He sent some companions to raise the money.

For thirty-eight days Caesar remained a captive, but he never cowered in fear. Instead he challenged the pirates, taking part in their games and sports as if he were their leader rather than a prisoner. When he wanted to sleep, he told them to be quiet. He often spent the hours writing poems and speeches that he read to the pirates. If they did not applaud, he called them savages to their faces. Moreover, he warned that he would return and take his revenge by crucifying them. The pirates did not take his threat seriously.

Soon his companions returned with the ransom, and Caesar was released. Immediately he commandeered a ship and crew and set out after the pirates. When Caesar caught up with them, he carried out his threat. However, Caesar ordered their throats slit before he crucified them so that they would not suffer long.

Caesar's future opponents could have learned from the pirates' fate. Many people would have reason to regret taking Julius Caesar too lightly. Decisiveness, speed, and ruthlessness were the hallmarks of his career as a soldier and a statesman.

Gaius Julius Caesar was born in 100 B.C. into the proud Julian clan that claimed descent from Venus and Aeneas. He grew up in a time of change and turmoil. The traditional Roman republic had depended on citizen-soldiers, who left their family farms to fight when they were needed. But the success of the Roman legions gradually changed the social structure. The people they conquered, in Italy and in other parts of the Mediterranean world, paid tribute to Rome in both grain and slaves. Wealthy Romans used the slaves to work large plantations, and Rome was no longer dependent on its small farmers for food. Forced off their land, the farmers moved to the city, where they searched for work.

The city became divided into factions—supporters of the rich (*equites*) or the poor (*populares*). To keep the populares satisfied, the government distributed free grain as a dole. Even so, fighting mobs frequently disturbed the city's peace. Sometimes a dictator was appointed to rule for a limited time. When one faction assumed power, partisans of the other were in danger of being killed. The Julian clan was allied with the populare forces and, as a young man, Julius was forced into exile for a time.

Julius realized that the republican form of government was no longer working. He yearned to do something about it and decided to enter politics. The young man was tall, fair, and well built. He had a wide face and penetrating dark brown eyes. But he suffered from epilepsy, which caused him suddenly to lapse into a coma or, at times, even to experience "fits" during which his muscles would twitch uncontrollably.

Few realized the depth of his ambition, for he seemed to be little more than a playboy. While other young men were winning fame as soldiers in Rome's endless conquests, Caesar was better known for his love affairs—some with older married women. He took great pains with his appearance, keeping his hair carefully trimmed and his face clean-shaven. In addition, Caesar had servants use tweezers to pluck out the hairs on his legs, arms, and chest. However, where he wished hair to grow—on his head—he soon lost it. His opponents enjoyed teasing him about his baldness, and he continually combed his remaining hair forward to try to hide it. He tried such remedies as crushed myrtle and bear grease, but no hair grew. A Roman historian wrote, "Of all the honors voted him by the Senate and People, none pleased him so much as the privilege of wearing a laurel wreath on all occasions." He could use it to conceal his baldness.

Caesar habitually wore clothing that made him stand out in a

crowd. He added wrist-length sleeves with fringes to his purple-striped tunic, loosely fastening his belt so that the tunic swirled. His dandyism deceived his political opponents. Cicero, a senator famous for his great speeches, distrusted Caesar. But even he once remarked, "When I see his hair so carefully arranged, and observe him adjusting it with one finger, I cannot imagine that it should enter such a man's thoughts to subvert the Roman state." Cicero was wrong. Julius Caesar would destroy the Roman republic.

People began to take notice when Caesar was elected to the post of Pontifex Maximus. His duties were to supervise all the sacred rituals in the city. The job was usually reserved for an older man, for the person who held it served for life. People thought that the vain, pleasure-seeking young man would be content with this post. It carried with it an official residence on the Sacred Way, the main road in the heart of Rome, and had few demanding duties. But for Caesar the office was only a steppingstone to higher things.

His fame rose when he served with the army in Spain. He gained a reputation for speed and skill in handling his troops. In administering the areas he controlled, Caesar was praised for his justice and fairness.

At the age of forty he returned to Rome, determined to make his play for power. In 60 B.C. Caesar secretly combined with two other men in what became known as the First Triumvirate. The other two were Pompey, the most famous general of the time, and Crassus, the richest man in Rome. Crassus had begun his career as chief of the city's fire department. When his forces arrived at a fire, Crassus would make an offer to buy the property. If the offer was turned down, his men let the fire burn. Crassus soon accumulated a great deal of property—at "fire sale" prices.

Caesar was certainly the junior partner in the Triumvirate, but he skillfully used his position to further his ambitions. He let the other two have the glory, but behind the scenes he controlled appointments to political offices and military commands. In this way he gained grateful allies in high places.

The following year Caesar used the connections of the two other triumvirs to get himself elected consul. After serving the one-year term, he requested the governorship of what was called Cisalpine Gaul. This was the area in today's northern Italy which includes the southern Alps. At that time, it was not regarded as part of Italy, for many of its inhabitants were Gauls, a Celtic people.

For the next nine years Caesar surprised his contemporaries by following an aggressive military policy. Caesar proved his military genius as one of the greatest generals of all time. He led his forces against the barbarian tribes to the north and conquered all of Gaul—an area that included today's France, Belgium, parts of Switzerland, and western Germany. He also crossed the English Channel and briefly invaded Britain twice.

Caesar's conquests spread Roman law, language, and government over a large part of western Europe. Such modern terms as *jury, magistrate, censor,* and *dictator* have come from Roman political institutions.

Caesar commanded three legions. The Roman legion was the basic unit of the Roman army. Each legion was a formidable fighting force of about 4,000 men. Soldiers wore heavy body armor; each man carried a small sword and two short spears called darts. The Roman troops were organized in highly mobile companies of 120 men. Rigidly trained, the men fought in lines about eight feet apart. The first line was made up of new recruits, the second of more experienced soldiers, leaving the hard-core veterans in the third line to protect the rear and push the others forward. As the men moved toward the enemy, they threw their darts and then drew their swords for hand-to-hand fighting.

Caesar's troops, drawn from the lower classes of Roman society, were devoted to him. They grew confident that his military skill would bring them victory, and they shared in the loot plundered from conquered enemies. Caesar, older than most of his soldiers, won their respect by marching with them, swimming the rivers they crossed, and eating what they ate. When Caesar led his forces into battle, he wore a blood-red tunic to let both friend and foe know who was the Roman leader.

In return, Caesar demanded that his men fight hard. Any stragglers or cowards faced severe punishment. Deserters were chased down and either placed in the front lines in the next battle, or executed, usually by crucifixion.

Caesar's success in Gaul increased his popularity in Rome. Crassus had been killed in a military campaign in today's northern Turkey. Pompey felt threatened by Caesar's growing power. When Caesar asked whether he could run for the consulship again while remaining in Gaul, Pompey refused and demanded that Caesar disband his troops. This news angered Caesar. "Now that I am the leading Roman of my day," he exclaimed, "it will be harder to put me down a peg than degrade me to the ranks."

Caesar decided that the time was ripe for him to seize power. He gathered his legions and marched south toward Rome. Caesar reached the Rubicon River, the border between Cisalpine Gaul and Italy. It was illegal for Roman troops to enter Italy without the consent of the Senate. As he stood looking across the river he had a vision. He saw a gigantic ghost playing a flute. Some shepherds gathered to listen and were joined by Caesar's troops. The spirit grabbed a trumpet from a soldier, blew a loud blast, and crossed the river. Caesar saw this as a good omen and with the words, "The die is cast" (the dice are rolling), forged across the river. Even today the expression "crossing the Rubicon" means a decision from which there is no turning back.

Caesar's battle-hardened troops cut through all military opposition. Pompey fled Rome. Caesar stopped there only long enough to empty the treasury. Then he pursued Pompey into Greece, where his former ally had assembled an army twice the size of Caesar's. But Pompey was not the general Caesar was, and at the Battle of Pharsalus, Caesar overwhelmed Pompey's forces. Pompey escaped and fled to Egypt. But the Egyptians were unwilling to back a loser and when Caesar arrived, Pompey's head was thrown on the beach as a greeting.

Egypt's young queen, Cleopatra, wished to use Caesar to

secure her power in Egypt. She hid herself inside a rolled-up rug and had a servant carry her to Caesar's quarters. When the servant laid the rug on the floor, the beautiful young woman slipped out. Caesar, according to a Roman historian, "was spellbound the moment he set eyes on her and she opened her mouth to speak."

Cleopatra took Caesar on a cruise down the Nile River. But when a revolt broke out in a Roman province in Asia Minor (Turkey), Caesar sped there with his troops. Within five days of entering the territory and an hour after joining battle, Caesar routed the enemy. Caesar's famous report on this Battle of Zela was short and to the point: *Veni, vidi, vici*—"I came, I saw, I conquered."

Caesar moved on to Africa and Spain, where he defeated the last of his opponents. Returning to Rome, he celebrated with the largest triumph ever held. A triumph was a public celebration of a Roman military victory. Caesar's soldiers marched through the streets with captives from the three known continents, Europe, Asia, and Africa. Horses pulled carts overflowing with looted treasures. Soldiers carried large banners painted with scenes of battles and towns in flames. The triumph went on for four days. Leading the procession was Caesar, his face painted red, wearing a gold helmet and dressed in the robes of Jupiter, the chief Roman god.

Caesar had reached his goal of absolute power. The Senate named him dictator, giving him the power to reorganize the government as he saw fit. He rewarded the veterans of his army by giving them lands. He began a vast program to rebuild Rome's slums, where the populares lived. Through his authority as Pontifex Maximus, he reformed the calendar, replacing it with the more accurate Egyptian one. He renamed one of the months, calling it July after himself. (The calendar year that Caesar created remains, with only a few changes, the one we use today.)

All these policies were popular, and Rome was grateful. The senators gave him more honors, including the right to wear the purple toga worn long ago by Roman kings. Statues of him were borne in processions and placed among the images of the gods in Roman temples. Anniversaries of his victories and his birthday became holidays. His image appeared on the coins, the first time any living Roman had been so honored. The practice of flipping a coin to make a decision dates from Caesar's reign. His prestige was so great that judges settled lawsuits by flipping a coin—if

Caesar's head landed face up (heads), it meant that he approved the judge's decision.

In 44 B.C. Caesar was named dictator for life, and his person was declared inviolable and sacred. Many senators, and others as well, feared that Caesar was making himself a king. Romans who loved their republic refused to stand by and see it being destroyed. Secretly, a group of senators plotted to kill him. They decided to strike on the Ides of March (March 15).

On March 14 Caesar dined with one of his generals. The table conversation turned to death. When asked how he would like to die, Caesar responded: "Suddenly." That night Caesar was restless. A sudden wind caused all the windows and doors of the house to burst open. As a believer in omens, Caesar regarded this as a bad sign. His wife Calpurnia dreamed that he would die and begged him not to leave the house the next day.

Still he wanted to attend an important meeting of the Senate that day, to be held in the porch of Pompey's Theater. Caesar had asked the Senate to legalize his use of the title *rex*, or king, outside of Italy. At eleven he arrived in front of the theater. Suddenly he felt someone tug on his toga from behind. As he turned, the conspirators struck. Twenty-three dagger thrusts brought down the great Caesar. His blood-spattered body fell right below the bust of his former enemy, Pompey.

The Ides of March, the most famous date in antiquity, did not restore the Republic. The followers of Caesar rose up and destroyed his enemies. In his will, Caesar had named his grand-nephew Octavian as his heir. Octavian at first ruled with two others in the Second Triumvirate. Then he assumed power on his own and received the title Augustus. He was the first of the Roman emperors.

Caesar's life and career have fascinated people for many centuries. Rome's greatest orator, Cicero, described Caesar as "an instrument of wrath, terrifying in his vigilance, swiftness, and energy." But writers in other ages made Caesar a hero. William Shakespeare, in his play *Julius Caesar*, called him "the noblest Roman of them all." His campaigns are still studied in virtually every military school in the world. His very name became a title for rulers, such as *czar* in Russia, *kaiser* in Germany, and *qaysar* in Arabic. The magnetism and dash of his personality have not been dimmed by the twenty centuries since his death.

THE GOSSIP COLUMNIST OF ROME— SUETONIUS

An oil lamp burned late into the night at the imperial palace in Rome. Suetonius, the secretary of the Emperor Hadrian, was studying the secret archives that had accumulated in dusty storerooms for a century. He took notes by pressing his sharp-pointed stylus into a soft wax tablet secured in a wooden frame. Every once in a while he used the stub end of the stylus to rub out his notations and start again. Later he would make a good copy in ink on papyrus. Suetonius was using this treasure-trove of material to write a book about the private lives of the emperors.

The year was around A.D. 120. The Republic was dead. In its place was the Roman Empire, with power concentrated in the hands of a single man. The emperor controlled the army and the civil servants. The once-proud Roman Senate no longer had a real role in governing, although it continued as a ceremonial body. Still, the early Roman emperors provided peace for Italy and the countries conquered by Rome. This *Pax Romana* lasted for two hundred years.

The accomplishments of these emperors are important. Any historian would love to be in Suetonius' place, with complete access to the imperial records. But Suetonius was not content with learning about the policies of Rome's rulers. He was interested in what they looked like, their personalities, and the scandals of their private lives. In short he had the same interests that gossip columnists have today. His book, *The Twelve Caesars*, allows us to peek into the past and get an unofficial look at the lives of the first emperors. And what lives they were!

Gaius Suetonius Tranquillus was born in Rome in A.D. 69. It was a tempestuous year—four different emperors held power at different times. Rome had no regular method of succession to the imperial throne. The first emperors had named family members as their successors, but later the throne fell to anyone who had the power to take it. Supreme power was tempting, but it was also precarious. Murder and treachery often paved the way for one emperor to follow another.

Suetonius's father served in the army of Otho, one of the four emperors of the year 69. The Suetonius family was moderately wealthy and young Gaius received a good education. The Rome in which he grew up was called *caput mundi*—the greatest city in the world. About one million people lived in an area of about eight square miles. "All roads lead to Rome," was the saying of the day, and into the city thronged people from all over the empire. On its streets the boy could hear Greek, Syriac, and Armenian, as well as Latin. Luxurious homes lined the hills. Farther down, *insulae*, or apartment houses (some seven stories high), teemed with the poorer residents. The emperors provided for the large number of unemployed by distributing free food.

Rome was much like a large modern city, and Roman writers wrote about it warts and all. The writer Juvenal warned, "You are a thoughtless fool, unmindful of sudden disaster, if you don't make your will before you go out to have dinner. There are as many deaths in the night as there are open windows where you pass by." For people threw their garbage, including the contents of chamber pots (toilets), into the street below.

Night and day the city was alive with activity and noise. Julius Caesar had ruled that carts could not use the streets by day, so at night the rattle of wheels kept people awake. Romans feared crime as much as the people of any modern city. Juvenal warned, "Shut up your house or your store; bolts and padlocks and bars will never keep out all the burglars, or a holdup man will do you in with a switchblade."

Even so the city had its pleasures, both civilized and barbaric. A trip to the public baths provided relaxation and the opportunity for a workout, for they were equipped like a modern health club. Men and women lifted weights, swam, or took vigorous massages. The elegant tiled baths offered a place for cultured people to lounge, read, and gossip.

Romans looking for greater excitement could go to huge

amphitheaters and circuses to watch day-long games. At the Circus Maximus, more than 150,000 spectators jammed into the bleachers to watch chariot races. When an official dropped a white cloth onto the sand-covered arena, four-horse chariots came hurtling out of their boxes. Seven times they circled the narrow field in the middle. People in the crowd cheered for favorite charioteers, urging them to claim the inside track.

The emperors provided such entertainment free for anyone who could squeeze inside. "Such a throng flocked to all these shows," recalled Suetonius, "that many strangers had to lodge in tents pitched…along the roads, and the press was often such that many were crushed to death." The races were also a place to meet young women. Ovid, another writer, gave this advice:

> Many are the opportunities that await you in the circus. No one will prevent you sitting next to a girl. Get as close to her as you can. That's easy enough, for the seating is cramped anyway. Find an excuse to talk to her….Ask her what horses are entering the ring and which one she fancies. Approve her choices….If, as likely, a speck of dust falls into her lap, brush it gently away; and even if no dust falls, pretend it has and brush her lap just the same. If her cloak trails on the ground gather up the hem and lift it from the dirt. She will certainly let you have a glimpse of her legs.

When Suetonius was a boy, the splendid Colosseum opened. People flocked inside to see wild beasts turned loose against each other. More exciting and brutal were the gladiator shows in which men fought both wild animals and other men. The successful gladiator was the sports hero of Roman society. As the show began, the contestants, dressed in purple and gold cloaks, rode in chariots around the arena. Then they marched toward the emperor's box and raised their right arms. "Hail, Emperor! We who are about to die salute you!" they shouted. Urged on by the crowd, the gladiators fought with swords, tridents, or nets and spears. When a wounded gladiator fell, all eyes turned to the emperor's box. If he turned his thumbs up, the injured gladiator was spared; thumbs down meant he would be slain at once.

Suetonius studied to be a lawyer. However, his heart was not in it, for he was not a good speaker. On one occasion, he excused his absence from court because he had a bad dream the night

before. His interests lay in writing, and as a young man he found a patron in the writer Pliny the Younger. Through him, Suetonius began to publish books on grammar and biographies of Roman writers. Pliny himself had a close relationship with the Emperor Trajan. When Trajan sent Pliny as an ambassador to Bithynia, a province in today's Turkey, Suetonius went along.

Here Suetonius came into contact with members of a new religion—Christianity. Pliny wrote letters to Trajan asking for guidance in dealing with the Christians. These followers of Jesus of Nazareth (a town in Syria Palestina, the southern part of the Roman province of Syria) refused to accept the official gods of Rome. Members of other religions were allowed to practice their faiths if they acknowledged the gods believed to be the support of the Roman Empire. Because Christians refused to do this, the state persecuted them.

Through Pliny, Suetonius later obtained a post at the emperor's palace in Rome. The next emperor, Hadrian, named Suetonius to be his secretary. In this position he traveled with the emperor on a tour throughout the empire. But soon after, Suetonius was disgraced by a scandal. All we know today is that Suetonius was dismissed along with others for incorrect conduct with the Empress Sabina. Unfortunately, Suetonius had no Suetonius to tell the tale.

Suetonius could now work full time on his book, *The Twelve Caesars*. It begins with Julius Caesar and continues through the emperors from Augustus to Domitian. From Augustus on,

Suetonius gleaned his tidbits from eyewitnesses and acquaintances of the emperors. Other historians describe Augustus' rise to power and his subtle manipulation of government. But Suetonius tells us that he wore long underwear. We learn that Augustus was very superstitious, believing it bad luck if he accidentally put his right foot into his left shoe in the morning. Augustus liked to start a journey when there was a drizzling rain, because he felt that it would ensure success and a speedy return. The most powerful man in the empire was afraid of thunder and lightning and carried a sealskin as a good-luck charm to ward off harm from storms.

The next emperor was Tiberius, the son of Augustus' wife Livia by an earlier marriage. Livia continually schemed to get Augustus to name Tiberius as his heir. Suetonius describes Tiberius as "so strong that he could poke a finger through a sound, newly-plucked apple or into the skull of a boy or young man. He had a handsome, fresh-complexioned face, though subject to occasional rashes of pimples."

Tiberius was incredibly stingy; he even put a stop to the giving of good-luck gifts for the New Year, an ancient Roman custom. (He also prohibited "promiscuous" kissing on the same day.) Tiberius' thrift grew to outlandish greed. He made subjects name him as beneficiaries in their wills and then forced them to commit suicide.

After some years as emperor, Tiberius tired of Rome. He moved to the Isle of Capri and spent his days in assorted cruelties. His final disservice to Rome was to name Caligula as his successor.

"Caligula the Monster" is what Suetonius called him. The young emperor insisted on being treated as a god, replacing the heads of statues of Jupiter and other gods with representations of his own face. People realized that he was crazy, but feared his wrath so much that they rushed to please his every whim. Suetonius wrote that Caligula

> established a shrine to himself as god, with priests...and a life-sized golden image of himself, which was dressed every day in clothes identical with those he happened to be wearing. All the richest citizens tried to gain priesthoods here, either by influence or bribery....During the day Caligula would carry on whispered conversations with [the statue of] Jupiter, pressing his ear to the god's mouth, and sometimes raising his voice in anger. Once he was overheard threatening the god: "If you do not raise me up to Heaven I will cast you down to Hell."

Caligula loved to play cruel jokes on his subjects. Outside a theater he scattered free tickets for the best seats, and then watched with glee as people fought with the nobles who had bought the seats earlier. At gladiator shows he would order soldiers to remove the awnings that shielded people from the sun at the hottest part of the day—and then forbid anyone to leave. Sometimes he would "stage comic duels between respectable householders who happened to be physically disabled in some way or other." Caligula frequently declared, "Let them hate me, so long as they fear me." But his cruelties became so reckless that his own guards finally killed him.

Caligula's successor was his uncle Claudius, who was lame and had a pronounced speech defect. But Claudius was a fine scholar whose only weakness was food. Suetonius wrote:

> No matter where Claudius happened to be, he always felt ready for food or drink. One day, while he was judging a case in Augustus's Forum, the delicious smell of cooking assailed his nostrils. He descended from the Tribunal, closed the court, and went to the dining room of the Leaping Priests in the near-by Temple of Mars, where he immediately took his place at the meal he had scented. It was seldom that Claudius left a dining-hall except gorged and sodden; he would then go to bed and sleep with his mouth wide open—thus allowing a feather to be put down his throat, which would bring up the superfluous food and drink as vomit.

Claudius unwisely married Agrippina, the sister of Caligula. She already had a son, Nero, by another man. Conniving to place Nero on the throne, she served Claudius a dish of poisoned mushrooms.

Nero turned out to be another monster. At his birth, friends congratulated his father, who responded that "any child born to himself and Agrippina was bound to have a detestable nature and become a public danger." When Nero became emperor, his mother thought he would be grateful. But after she started to tell him what to do, he decided to kill her. It was no easy task!

Suetonius wrote:

> [Nero] tried to poison her three times, but she had always taken the antidote in advance; so he rigged up a machine in the ceiling of her bedroom which would dislodge the panels and drop them on her while she slept. However, someone gave the

secret away. Then he had a collapsible cabin-boat designed which would either sink or fall in on top of her. Pretending to want to make up with her, he sent the most friendly note inviting her to celebrate the Feast of Minerva with him, and on her arrival made one of his captains stage an accidental collision with the galley in which she had sailed. Then he postponed the feast until a late hour, and when at last she said: "I really must get back," offered her his collapsible boat instead of the damaged galley. Nero was in a very happy mood as he led Agrippina down to the dock....He sat up all night waiting anxiously for news of her death. At dawn Lucius Agermus, her freedman, entered joyfully to report that although the ship had sunk, his mother had swum to safety, and Nero need have no fear on her account.

In desperation, Nero finally hired a professional assassin to stab his mother to death.

Nero regarded himself as a talented actor and singer. Nothing could so advance a man's career as praise for Nero's "genius." He loved to give public performances, where the audiences squirmed for hours. Suetonius reported:

No one was allowed to leave the theater during his recitals, however pressing the reason, and the gates were kept barred. We read of women in the audience giving birth, and of men being so bored with the music and the applause that they furtively dropped down from the wall at the rear, or pretended to be dead and were carried away for burial.

The Romans finally tired of Nero, and he committed suicide as soldiers moved in to kill him. Nero's last line was "Dead! And so great an artist!"

Four emperors followed in rapid succession in the year 69. They included Otho, who ruled only ninety-five days. Suetonius learned from his father, one of Otho's soldiers, that the emperor "did not look like a very courageous man." Otho had the hair of his entire body removed and wore "a well-made toupee." Otho shaved frequently and since his boyhood had applied moist bread to his face to prevent his beard from growing.

Vespasian was the first of the three Flavian emperors: himself and his two sons. They complete the story that Suetonius tells. Vespasian appears to have been the only emperor with a sense of humor. He always liked a joke. His son Titus complained because

Vespasian had placed a tax on the contents of the city's urinals (used to clean wool before weaving). Vespasian handed his son a gold coin that had come from the tax. "Does it smell bad, my son?" he asked. "No, Father!" Titus replied. "That's odd: it comes straight from the urinal!" Even on his deathbed, Vespasian quipped: "Dear me! I must be turning into a god."

Titus succeeded him, and it is remarkable that Suetonius has almost nothing bad to say about him. However, Titus' reign was marked by natural disasters, including a fire in Rome that burned for three days and nights, and an outbreak of plague. "Throughout these frightful disasters," Suetonius said, "Titus showed far more than an Emperor's concern; it resembled the deep love of a father for his children." Titus contributed a fortune of his own money to help the suffering and repair the city. He offered sacrifices to the gods to beg them to end the plague.

One of the disasters of Titus' reign included the eruption of Mount Vesuvius, south of Naples, in the year A.D. 79. The volcano's lava buried the city of Pompeii. Archaeologists, who began excavating in the 1760s, have found a virtually complete Roman city preserved in the hardened lava and have learned much about Roman daily life from it.

Suetonius had little respect for Titus' brother Domitian, who succeeded him. Domitian pleased the Romans by presenting spectacular entertainments. They included a sea battle for which the Colosseum was flooded and even torch-lit gladiator shows at night. Women gladiators were introduced for the first time. Domitian reduced the number of laps in the chariot races from seven to five, so that 100 races could be held in a single day.

However, Domitian became a sadistic monster. Suetonius writes that he "would spend hours alone every day catching flies— believe it or not!—and stabbing them with a needle-sharp pen. Once, on being asked whether anyone was with the emperor, his secretary answered wittily: 'No, not even a fly.'" His long-suffering wife took part in the plot that assassinated him.

Suetonius' record of the emperors makes us wonder how Rome's government functioned at all. Still, his tale of the vices and follies of Rome has been enjoyed by generations of readers. This little sample gives only a taste of the riches of his book.

TROUBADOUR OF GOD—
ST. FRANCIS OF ASSISI

Around the year 1205, a slight, unimpressive-looking, twenty-four-year-old man sat in a courtroom in Assisi, a town in central Italy. The young man was the defendant in an unusual court case. His father, Piero Bernardone, a wealthy cloth merchant, was suing his own son to regain some lost property.

Francis, the son, admitted that he had sold some of his father's merchandise, along with a horse. But he had a good reason. When Francis had visited the rundown little church of San Damiano, the statue of Christ on the crucifix above the altar spoke to him. Christ had said, "Go, Francis, and repair my house, which, as you see, is well-nigh in ruins."

Francis had immediately gone home and taken his father's goods and horse. However, after he sold them, the priest at the small church had refused to accept the money. Francis still had it in his possession.

Then, to the astonishment of the crowd in court, Francis stripped to his hair shirt. He returned all the money along with his clothes—for those too had been a gift from his father. The plaintiff, or suer, had won the case but had lost his son. "From now on," Francis said, "I shall serve one father only—God."

The bishop who presided over the trial offered him a shabby woolen cloak. After marking it with a cross, Francis put it on. Happily, he went on his way to a new life. Thus began a new kind of religious order and the career of one of the most beloved figures of history—Francis of Assisi.

At his birth Francis was baptized with the name John. His father shared in the new wealth and trade that spread through the cities of Italy in the eleventh and twelfth centuries. But young John preferred reading poetry to learning how to keep the account books of his father's business. He took after his mother, a vivacious woman from the south of France. She taught him the songs of the troubadours, wandering poets of her homeland who sang about women they loved. Young John so loved the French troubadours' poems that people started to call him Francis.

Francis was a lively child with many friends. In his young manhood, he joined other youths in a series of wild escapades. In 1202 he joined a raiding party on the neighboring town of Perugia, for which he spent a year in jail. But after an illness Francis experienced a complete change of heart. One night after a party, a friend discovered him sitting and staring at the sky. His companion quipped: "What's the matter, Francis? Have you gotten married?"

"Yes," responded Francis, "to the fairest of all brides, to the Lady Poverty." From that time, Francis decided to dedicate his life to helping the poor. Shortly afterward he heard Christ's voice, leading to the "theft" of the bolts of cloth from his father's shop.

After Francis left Assisi, he lived for a while in a hut just outside the town. Called *Poverello* ("Little Poor Man"), he soon collected a band of followers. They began to wander from place to place, working in the fields or taking odd jobs. When they could not find work, they begged for their meals. They slept in barns or in the fields when they had to.

Sometimes they shared the huts of lepers, who were shunned by everyone else. As a youth, Francis had always feared lepers, who had a disease that caused their skin to disintegrate. Now he forced himself to kiss their hands, to show that they were as beloved as any of God's creatures.

Sleeping in the open was no hardship for Francis. For it brought him close to the natural world, which he felt God had created out of love. Because the animals depended on God for their sustenance, he felt a deep kinship with them. It was said that birds and even crickets came to sing just for him and that once he tamed a wild wolf by speaking sternly to it.

Francis wished to imitate the life of Christ as closely as possible. He believed that only those who had stood barefoot in the marketplace begging alms could understand the poverty of others. By renouncing all material wealth and property, he and his companions found freedom and happiness. They displayed such joy that they were called *Joculatores Domini* (God's jesters). In 1209, he and eleven companions journeyed to Rome to ask the pope to approve their rule of poverty and good works to the poor. Innocent III, one of the most powerful popes of the Middle Ages, hesitated. Francis and his companions were not like any other religious order. None were priests or trained in theology. Still, there was work for the Church in the growing towns and cities of Italy. The pope granted Francis' followers the right to be known as *fratres minores* (lesser brothers), wear a gray habit, and go barefoot. They could counsel people but were not to become involved in theological issues.

Francis went out to the towns and cities of Italy with verve and love. He drew people to him with the sweetness of his personality, and soon many others joined his group. Other religious orders established monasteries, which were open to poor people seeking refuge. But the Franciscans went to the people, wherever they lived.

Although he was a layman (not a priest), Francis began to preach to others. Parish priests said Mass and preached sermons in Latin, which by Francis' time was not understood by the common people. Their spoken language was becoming more like today's Italian. When Francis preached, he used the language that everyone could understand.

Francis described Jesus as a man who had gone into the world and associated with real people. Francis emphasized that Jesus was a carpenter and his apostles simple fishermen, people whom the poor could identify with. Francis' influence was so strong that artists soon took up a new way of painting Jesus—as a more human figure. Formerly, religious art showed Jesus as a divine ruler.

One year when Francis was preaching at the Christmas season, he carved a figure of the infant Jesus and placed it in a crib surrounded by figures of Mary, Joseph, and farm animals. This was the first creche, now a part of Christmas celebrations everywhere.

Francis sometimes struggled with his desires. Although Lady Poverty remained his ideal, he was often lonely and longed for the pleasures of a family. One winter, while he was preaching in the Apennines, the mountains that run down the spine of Italy, he built himself a family of snow people.

He kept his love of song and poetry. He would take two sticks and make the motions of playing the violin while singing one of his beloved troubadour songs. Now as a preacher, however, he was a troubadour of God rather than of romance.

While preaching in Assisi in 1212, he inspired a childhood friend with his love for the poor. She was seventeen-year-old Clare, the daughter of a rich family that had made plans for her to marry a suitable husband. But one night she slipped away to join Francis at his hut. He gave her a coarse cloth habit and cut off her hair. Then he took her to live with Benedictine nuns in a nearby convent. This was the start of the Poor Clares, the women's branch of the Franciscans.

Later Clare's widowed mother and some other women joined her. They agreed to live in complete poverty according to Franciscan principles. Clare's followers spent much of their time in prayer, hoping to bring a new awareness of God to the world. The people of Assisi believed that Clare's holiness had twice saved them from foreign armies that had marched on the city, and then turned away. The Abbess Clare remained a close friend of Francis to the end of his life. He often turned to her for wise and affectionate counsel.

Wanting to spread his work beyond Italy, Francis traveled to France. When he heard that Christian crusaders were battling Muslims in Egypt, he boarded a ship and joined them. After being warmly welcomed in the Christian camp, he walked across to the Muslim side. This took great courage because the sultan, the ruler of Egypt, ordered any Christian captive put to death.

The Muslim soldiers attacked him, but Francis kept shouting, "Sultan! Sultan!" Puzzled, the soldiers took him to the court. The sultan agreed to listen to Francis preach. Although he did not convince the sultan that Christianity was better than Islam, his devotion and holiness were impressive. The sultan invited Francis to remain in Egypt, but Francis declined and returned to Italy.

Here he found that as his order had grown, problems had arisen. Many of the Franciscans did not find Lady Poverty as important as he did. Pious rich people had donated estates, houses, and money to carry on the Franciscans' work. Francis felt that all such gifts should be refused. Others disagreed. Now that God had provided for them, why not use these gifts to help the poor? The Franciscans could build monasteries with farms and libraries, as other religious orders did. There were too many members to depend solely on begging.

Francis was dismayed by the controversy. He wished to follow the simple rule of poverty that he had written. Since others did not, he chose to resign as head of the order. "Lord, I give you back this family which you entrusted to me," he said.

He built himself a hut where he could live alone and pray. One morning when he arose from his knees after a long night of prayer, he noticed wounds on his hands and feet, like those Jesus had suffered on the cross. Unwilling to call attention to them, Francis covered them by wearing socks and long sleeves. People noticed though that Francis no longer went barefoot as he always had before. Soon the story spread, and people became convinced that the stigmata, as such wounds are called, were an additional sign of Francis' holiness.

Yet the wounds were painful and made it difficult for Francis to walk. He continued preaching anyway, using a donkey to get from place to place. Legends spread that Francis could cure the sick as Jesus did. People offered him loaves of bread to bless, and kept them to eat when they fell ill.

But Francis himself was not well, even though he was only about forty years old. Years of sleeping in the open, of denying himself food for days on end, had taken their toll. He sometimes apologized to his own body, which he called "Brother Ass," for treating it so badly.

Tired and sick, Francis went to Clare's convent of San Damiano in Assisi. The nuns prepared a special hut of reeds for him in the vineyard on the grounds. The shelter was soon swarming with mice who ran all over him, but he refused to chase them out.

Francis gave thanks for the beauties of nature and God. Like the troubadours he admired, he wrote poems and songs about the things he most loved. His "Canticle of the Sun" is the first recorded poem written in Italian, rather than Latin:

> Praise to you, my Lord, and all your creatures,
> Particularly Brother Sun
> Who rules the Day and gives us light from you,
> And is beautiful and radiant in his splendor.
> From you, Most High, he takes his power.
> Be praised, my Lord, by Sister Moon and the Stars
> You made in Heaven, luminous and precious,
> Be praised, My Lord, by Brother Wind and by the Air,
> And every kind of Weather, clouded or fine,
> By which you give sustenance to your creatures.
> Be praised, my Lord, by Sister Water,
> Which is very useful and humble and precious and
>   chaste.
> Be praised, my Lord, by Brother Fire,
> Through whom you brighten the night,
> And he is beautiful and cheerful and strong.
> Be praised, my Lord, by our mother, Sister Earth,
>   who feeds and governs us,
> And brings forth many kinds of fruit, and flowers of
>   many colors and herbs.
> Praise ye and bless the Lord, give thanks,
> And serve him with humility.

Feeling "Sister Death" approaching, Francis returned to the old hut he had lived in when he left Assisi. There, surrounded by friends and the memories of his life, he died in the year 1226. It was said that a flock of doves rose from the roof as if they were accompanying his soul to Heaven. In less than two years, he was canonized as a saint by the Roman Catholic Church. He remains one of the most beloved people who ever lived.

THE POWER OF LOVE—DANTE

On May 1, 1274, in the prosperous city of Florence, a nine-year-old boy named Dante Alighieri went to a party. A neighbor had invited his friends and their children to celebrate the beginning of spring. Flowers were scattered throughout the house, candies and treats were set out, and Dante played happily with the other children, including the neighbor's daughter, eight-year-old Beatrice Portinari.

Young though he was, Dante fell head over heels in love. Years later, he would recall the "noble color" of Beatrice's dress—"a subdued and excellent crimson…At that moment I truly say that the spirit of life, which dwells in the innermost chamber of the heart, began to tremble so violently that the least pulses of my body shook with it."

What makes this childhood love so important more than seven hundred years later? It is simply that Beatrice served as Dante's inspiration for one of the greatest poems ever written, *The Divine Comedy*. The name of Dante is celebrated not only in Italy, but all over the world—and it will forever be linked with the name of that little girl Beatrice.

Durante Alighieri was born in Florence in May 1265, the son of Alighiero di Bellincione and his wife Bella. The Alighieri family led a comfortable life, for Dante's father and grandfather were money lenders, the bankers of the day. Florence, "the city of flowers," was a rich city-state located on the Arno River. The city's wealth was growing by leaps and bounds because it was a center of cloth-making. Florence's bankers, like the Alighieris, began to make fortunes lending money to people who wanted to buy wool to make cloth.

The child soon became known affectionately as Dante, a nickname meaning "he who gives." A year after his birth he was baptized at Florence's pride and joy—the "Baptistery," the church of

San Giovanni Battista (St. John the Baptist), the city's patron saint. All the children born in the past year were baptized on St. John's feast day in February. Dante's parents placed a black bean in the baptismal font that served as a kind of census roll. (White beans were placed for girls.)

Dante's mother died when he was a small child, and his father remarried. Dante's closest companion in childhood was his older sister. Dante went to school as did most of the boys and girls of Florence. He studied Latin, public speaking, and philosophy. An avid student, Dante read so much that he may have damaged his eyesight. He said he could only see the stars "blurred by a white mist." Probably he was merely nearsighted.

Dante and his fellow-students were part of a reawakening of Italian scholarship and art. He devoted himself to the study of the Latin poet Virgil and other classical authors. In Dante's youth, Florence was becoming a center of Italian culture. In the centuries that followed, it would be one of the most glorious cities in the world. Wealthy families built magnificent *palazzos* for themselves and contributed money to construct beautiful churches. They supported the work of poets, scholars, and artists.

One of these young artists was Giotto, born in the nearby city of Vespignano. Giotto began the style of realistic painting that two centuries later influenced the great artists of the Renaissance. Giotto is thought to have made the only drawing that exists of Dante as a youth. It shows a lean-faced man with a bony nose, wearing the stocking cap that was then in fashion among students.

Dante was still obsessed with his beloved Beatrice. Nine years after their first meeting, he saw her again. This time she was dressed in white, walking in the street with another woman. He wrote that "she turned her eyes toward the place where I most timidly stood, and in her indescribable courtesy saluted me so graciously that at that moment I seemed to see the heights of blessedness."

He probably worked up the courage to speak to her but was afraid to declare his love. Instead, he pretended to be in love with two other women by writing poems for them. Beatrice probably heard of his poems, but her reaction was not what Dante hoped for. When he saw Beatrice a third time, she publicly snubbed him in the street.

Dante was crushed. Afterward, he had a vision that predicted an early death for his beloved. When she died in 1290 at the age of twenty-three or twenty-four, and Dante was overcome with grief. He was comforted only by the belief that she had instantly been carried "to heaven on high, to that kingdom where the angels live in peace." In death Beatrice became Dante's muse, or inspiration, for his poetry.

From this experience Dante wrote poems of love in what he called the "sweet new style." He collected them together in his first book, *Vita Nuova* (The New Life.) It described the stages of his love for "a wonderful lady." This love poetry was a great success, for it was written in the everyday language of Dante's Florence.

All his life, Dante had a hot temper. One story about him relates that he heard a blacksmith singing his poems while hammering on his anvil. Dante stopped to listen. But he realized that the smith sometimes substituted his own words in place of the ones Dante had written. Dante went into the man's forge and began to throw his tools into the street. The blacksmith rushed to stop him, and Dante said, "If you do not want me to spoil your things, do not spoil mine."

"What of yours am I spoiling?" said the smith. "You sing out of my book," said Dante, "and do not give the words as I wrote them. That is my business, and you are spoiling it for me." The next time the blacksmith wanted to sing, he chose another poem.

Dante was devoted to his native city. In 1287 he fought with Florence's army in a war against the neighboring town of Arezzo. Six hundred horsemen, with Dante in the front row, rode forward with the red lily flag of Florence flying overhead. On the plain of Campaldino, enemy soldiers rushed against them with spears and lances. The battle raged all day long, but at the end the Florentines were victorious. Later Dante would write about the Battle of Campaldino in his epic poem.

He became involved in the complicated politics of his city. Florence's government was dominated by the guilds—groups of craftsmen who banded together to increase their power. Dante enrolled in the Guild of Physicians and Apothecaries. It included not only merchants of spices and drugs, but also jewelers, painters, and booksellers. Hand-copied books were part of the wares to be found in an apothecary shop, what is now called a drug store or pharmacy. In 1300 Dante was elected to a two-month term as one of the six priors who governed the city. He was then thirty-five years old.

By that time he had also married a woman named Gemma, who belonged to one of the noble families of Florence. The couple would have four children, two boys and two girls. Dante sometimes neglected his wife, staying up very late studying his books. But apparently she became used to his strange habits, and their marriage was a happy one.

Dante had the misfortune of serving as prior of the city during a violent rivalry between two noble families. Their supporters became known as "Whites" and "Blacks." Dante was among the Whites. To try to halt the fighting that broke out between the two groups, the priors exiled some of the participants from both sides. Dante agreed with the decision, though one of the exiles was his best friend, a poet named Cavalcanti. Dante, however, had earned the hatred of the Blacks.

The fighting did not stop. The Blacks were allied with the pope, Boniface VIII. Seeing a chance to increase his influence, Boniface asked a prince of France, Charles of Valois, to lead an army against Florence. As Charles' army approached, Dante and three other Whites went to Rome in October 1301 to negotiate with the pope. But Charles captured Florence and forced the Whites out of the city. Dante was ordered not to return for two years. When Dante unwisely criticized the pope, he was sentenced to be burned alive if he ever came back to Florence. He would never see the city of his birth again.

Exiled, Dante entered a life of wandering from place to place. Scholars and writers could find work at the courts of princes and dukes. However, Dante's quick tongue often got him into trouble. One of the rich lords who employed him pointed out that the court jester was well-liked, while Dante was not. "I wonder," the lord said, "how it is that this man, fool though he be, understands how to please us all, while you, for all your reputed wisdom, can do nothing of the kind."

Dante sarcastically replied, "You would hardly wonder at that, if you remembered that like manners and like minds are the real causes of friendship." In other words, the lord was as big a fool as his jester.

Dante's great dream was to see Italy reunited under a new emperor. The glory of ancient Rome had continued to be admired centuries after the breakup of the empire. Centuries before Dante, a king named Charlemagne controlled most of today's France, Germany, Belgium, and northern Italy. In the year 800 the pope crowned Charlemagne emperor, linking the religious prestige of the Church to the political power of the new emperor. However, Charlemagne's empire was divided among his three sons after his death. A German king, Otto I, named himself emperor in 861. His successors often interfered in Italian affairs. By Dante's time, the title of Holy Roman Emperor had passed to a new ruler, named Henry. Dante wrote a letter urging Henry to bring Italy into a "universal monarchy" that would include most of Europe. When Henry died, Dante's plans were shattered. (But as will be seen in later chapters, the Holy Roman Emperors would continue to send their armies into Italy, with disastrous results.)

During his wanderings, Dante had been thinking about his own masterpiece, which he had already begun. His wife, left behind in Florence, found some puzzling sheets of paper in their home. They were the beginning of the poem, in which the author (never named in the poem) finds himself lost in a dark forest. He is unable to climb a mountain, because three beasts bar his way: a leopard, a lion, and a wolf. (They stand for lust, pride, and greed—perhaps the three sins Dante felt were responsible for his suffering.)

The author then meets the greatest Roman poet, Virgil, who offers to show Dante the way to salvation. They begin with a tour of Hell. In Virgil's *Aeneid*, the hero Aeneas had descended into the underworld during his wanderings, and Dante patterned his own masterpiece on Virgil's.

Dante's wife sent the manuscript to her husband. He was then living at the castle of an old friend who had fought alongside him at the Battle of Campaldino. When Dante received the manuscript, he apparently set out to finish it. The year was 1307.

His travels were not over. No one is really sure where he spent much of the next ten years, living on the charity of friends while he carried with him the manuscript that he was shaping into one of the world's greatest poems. He had one last chance to return to Florence. The city offered amnesty to any remaining exiles, on condition that they pay a fine and offer themselves at the Church of

San Giovanni Battista. The penitent exiles had to dress in sack-cloth, with a paper hat on their heads.

Dante refused to humiliate himself in such a way. He wrote to a relative in Florence, "Besides, what does it matter? Wherever I am, can I not contemplate the sun and the stars and meditate under the vault of Heaven on those truths which are so sweet to me?"

In 1317 Dante found his final home—the city of Ravenna, whose ruler kept a strict neutrality in the quarrels among the other city-states. Three of Dante's children, Jacopo, Pietro, and Antonia, joined him at Ravenna. (Antonia became a nun, taking the name Beatrice.) Here, Dante completed his great work, the 14,233 lines of poetry that have fascinated readers ever since.

The work we know as *The Divine Comedy* is a Christian guide-book that leads a pilgrim from the torment and pain of the damned

to divine salvation. Dante takes the reader through the worlds of the afterlife—Hell, Purgatory, and Heaven. He makes the journey seem very real—so much so that people who read it believed he had magically visited those three supernatural regions. One day when he was walking through Ravenna, a woman pointed him out, saying, "See how his beard is frizzled and how dark his complexion is from the smoke and heat that are down below?"

And Dante took his revenge on the enemies who had tormented him. He placed many of them, including popes, in the depths of Hell. Those he loved and respected, of course, he found in Heaven.

Because he depicts the torments of Hell so realistically, the first part of his poem, *Inferno*, has always been the most popular. The poet and Virgil enter Hell through a gate over which are inscribed the words: *Lasciate Ogni Speranza, Voi Ch'Entrate* ("Abandon All Hope, You Who Enter.")

Hell is a funnel-shaped kingdom with nine levels going down into the center of the earth. The farther Dante descends, the greater the sinners and the worse the punishments. Hell contains torrid deserts, cities aflame, and burning rivers. Throughout the journey Dante hears the screams and laments of the damned. There are many kinds of punishments. Some sinners are boiling in tar. Others have been split in half but remain alive. Some have been turned into trees. When Dante breaks off a branch, it bleeds.

Farther down, he sees the heads of corrupt priests sticking up from the burning earth. From some holes, only feet appear—belonging to sinful popes who are buried head downward. Along the way Dante meets Florentines who ask for news of their city. At the very bottom Dante finds Satan himself, a hideous monster with three faces and six flapping bat wings. In each of Satan's mouths, his sharp teeth chew the sinners Dante thought worst—Judas, the betrayer of Christ, and Brutus and Cassius, the two who struck the first blows to kill Julius Caesar.

After clambering over Satan, Virgil and Dante come out on the other side of the earth. On an island they see the mountain of Purgatory reaching upward. Purgatory has seven levels, corresponding to each of the seven deadly sins from pride to lust. Here, sinners repent of their sins to make them worthy of Heaven or Paradise. As Dante reaches the top, Virgil disappears. As a pagan, Virgil cannot enter Paradise.

Alone, Dante is frightened. But then he hears a familiar voice calling his name. He sees Beatrice, who will be his new guide. They rise into the air to the sounds of celestial music. Dante is disturbed by his weightlessness. But Beatrice explains: "You are not on earth! Lightning never moved so fast as you are moving now." They stop on the moon and look down on the earth. Dante is struck by its "miserable appearance."

Heaven has ten levels. The Europeans of Dante's time thought that all the objects in the sky revolved around the earth. The moon was nearest, followed by the sun and the five planets that are visible without a telescope, the stars, and finally the darkness beyond. Dante proceeds through all these, finally reaching the tenth ring. There, he sees a blinding vision of God—"the Supreme Light." To describe it is beyond the power of any poet, but Dante calls it "the Love that moves the sun and the other stars."

Europeans had no printing presses in Dante's time, but friends made copies of the parts of his poem as he finished them. Because Dante wrote in Italian, not Latin, his work soon became very popular. Even people who could not read, heard it read aloud and were thrilled by the music of his language, the vivid descriptions of scenes and characters, and finally his great message of hope and salvation.

Dante died at the age of fifty-two, still in exile in Ravenna. As his fame grew after his death, Florence decided that it wanted the famous exile to come back. Century after century, Florence demanded that Ravenna return Dante's body to his native city. At one point, a pope commanded that Dante's tomb be opened. But nothing was inside; monks had hidden his bones. Today, Dante still rests in Ravenna.

His work began the great tradition of Italian literature. Inspired by his achievement, others felt it was no longer necessary to write in the language of the ancient Romans. A new tradition of art and culture was beginning. Yet no Italian writer and few in other languages would ever equal the greatness of the man who spent his life looking for a home. Inspired by the love he first felt as a boy, he wrote an epic of the triumph of love over the sufferings and sorrows of this world.

CHAPTER 5

WOMEN IN A MAN'S WORLD— ISABELLA AND BEATRICE D'ESTE

On January 22, 1491, fifteen-year-old Beatrice d'Este rode into the city of Milan. A hundred trumpeters rode ahead of her to announce the arrival of the new bride of Milan's leading citizen, thirty-nine-year-old Ludovico Sforza. Red and blue satin ribbons, the colors of the Sforza family, hung from every window and doorway. Crowds lined the streets, eager to see Ludovico's young bride and the richly attired nobles and ambassadors who had come from all over Italy for the celebration.

Ludovico, known to everyone as *Il Moro* ("the Moor") because of his dark complexion, wore a suit of spun gold cloth. With his bride on his arm, he mounted a platform to watch knights from the many Italian cities compete in a tournament. Beatrice's relatives arrived in a cart drawn by stags and "unicorns," the animals on the d'Este family crest. At the end came a group of twelve riders wearing on their helmets a Moor's head, the personal symbol of Il Moro.

Suddenly, a troop of "wild Scythians" galloped into the square. As the crowd gasped, they rushed toward the platform. Reining in their horses, they threw off their costumes, revealing themselves as captains of the Milanese army. Their leader thrust a golden lance into the ground, and a huge dark man—a real Moor—stepped forward to recite a poem in honor of Beatrice.

Five days earlier, on a date chosen by Ludovico's personal astrologer, he and Beatrice had been married at the Sforza ancestral home in Pavia. It was the first time Beatrice had ever seen her husband. Among those in attendance was her elder sister Isabella, who was famed for her beauty and brains.

Some thought that Isabella would have made a better wife for the ambitious Ludovico than Beatrice. In fact, Milan might actually have celebrated Isabella's wedding that day, except for a stroke of fate ten years earlier.

Isabella and Beatrice were the eldest children of Ercole, the duke of Ferrara, a small but wealthy state located strategically between Venice and Milan. His family, the d'Este, had ruled Ferrara since the thirteenth century. Duke Ercole brought to the city's university some of the best scholars of the time. For in the 1400s a new mood of confidence and desire for learning swept Italy. A rebirth of interest in the classical learning of Greece and Rome gave the period the name Renaissance. Like other Renaissance princes, Ercole added to his city's glory by building grand churches and monasteries. He constructed a park where gazelles, antelopes, and giraffes roamed freely.

In 1473 Ercole married Eleanora, the daughter of King Ferrante of Naples. On May 18, 1474, she gave birth to a daughter, Isabella, and the city rejoiced. However, the following June, when a second daughter was born, a chronicler of the time wrote: "There were no rejoicings, because everyone wished for a boy." This daughter, of course, was Beatrice.

The gloom turned to joy in another year when a third child, Alfonso, was born. At last the duke had a son, but in the violent world of fifteenth-century Italy, that did not guarantee security for his reign. A few days after Alfonso's birth, Duke Ercole left the city. One of his nephews, Niccolo, seized the opportunity to raise a rebellion. Niccolo tried to capture Duchess Eleanora and her three children. However, she foiled the plot by carrying them to safety through a secret passageway in the palazzo. When the duke returned and restored order, he executed Niccolo and two hundred conspirators. By the standards of the time, this was not particularly harsh. To keep power and respect, princes often had to show what the price of disloyalty would be.

Eleanora took her daughters south to Naples to attend the wedding of her father, King Ferrante, whose first wife had died. Beatrice stayed there for the next eight years, in the care of her grandfather. She developed into a spoiled, yet beloved child. Although her grandfather was a cruel and harsh ruler, he doted on Beatrice, granting her every wish. He provided her with tutors who encouraged her love of music and dance. She performed her little dance steps for her grandfather almost as soon as she could walk, and learned to play many instruments, including the clavichord, an early type of piano. Beatrice kept seamstresses busy, for she was fond of adorning herself in the newest fashions of the day.

Back in Ferrara, Isabella had her own tutors. She too learned the skills of dance and music that would enable her to please a husband someday. Duke Ercole also saw to it that she learned to read and write Latin, Italian, and Spanish. One of her tutors recalled with pleasure hearing the young girl read aloud Virgil's *Aeneid*.

Isabella also listened as the duke's advisers discussed the twists and turns of politics. Each of the states of Italy jockeyed for advantage in the endless wars for influence and territory. Five states—Venice, Milan, Florence, Naples, and the Papal States— formed the great powers of the peninsula. As the ruler of a smaller state, Duke Ercole had to choose allies carefully, to help him keep his hold on Ferrara. His two daughters were pawns to use in the game of making alliances.

Mantua, a neighboring state, was ruled by the Gonzaga family. In 1480 the duke of Mantua sent an ambassador to negotiate a marriage between his son Francesco and Isabella d'Este. After the ambassador saw the little girl, he reported home with excitement:

> I...asked her questions on different subjects, to all of which she replied with such good sense and so ready a tongue that I marveled that a child of six could give such intelligent answers. I had heard about her singular intelligence, yet I would not have believed the extent of it.

Duke Ercole agreed to the marriage proposal. Just a few days before the official announcement, however, he received a second offer. Ludovico Sforza of Milan asked him for Isabella's hand.

Ercole must have been tempted. Ludovico was the uncle of the duke of Milan, but the young duke was only a tool in his uncle's hands. Everyone knew that Milan was under Ludovico's control. Still, Duke Ercole did not want to offend Mantua. So he offered his second daughter, Beatrice, to Ludovico. The offer was accepted.

Thus it was that ten years later Beatrice rode into Milan with Ludovico at her side. The festivities that followed were a foretaste of the life of splendor that awaited her.

Ludovico was one of the richest men in all Europe. Il Moro's court attracted singers, musicians, artists, architects, and scholars. Leonardo da Vinci had designed the costumes and decorations for the wedding party of Ludovico and Beatrice. Beatrice clapped her hands with delight as her husband showed her the Sforza treasure-room. It contained rare books bound in gold-and-jewel-encrusted covers, and fabulous gems such as a ruby called *El Spigo* (the ear of corn). It was said to be worth 250,000 ducats, roughly one-fourth of the annual income of the king of France.

Truly, the Sforzas lived like kings. After a later visit Isabella enviously told her husband: "Would to God that we, who are so fond of spending money, possessed as much!" Beatrice had a wardrobe of hundreds of dresses, jackets, furs, hats—all made of the finest cloth and decorated with jewels and embroidery.

The two sisters often wrote letters and visited each other. Both loved to hunt, and Isabella described a party outside Milan:

> We went out hunting in a beautiful valley which seemed as if it were expressly created for the spectacle. All the stags were driven into the wooded valley . . . so that they were forced to swim the river . . . where the ladies watched them from under the pergola and green tents set up on the hillside . . . but only two [stags] climbed the hillside and ran far out of sight, so that we did not see them killed . . . Many wild boars and goats were found, but only one boar was killed before our eyes, and one wild goat, which fell to my share. Last of all came a wolf, which made fine somersaults in the air as it ran past us, and amused the whole company . . . . And so, with much laughter and merriment, we returned home, to end the day at supper.

Beatrice was fond of pranks. On one occasion, she and her maids disguised themselves in ordinary dress to walk through the city. They got into a fight with some women who insulted them, and came home with their clothes torn and spattered with mud. When her sister heard of this escapade, she wrote: "When I read

your letter...I could see the angry flash in your eye, and hear the indignant answer that you would have had...for anyone who dared insult you."

Isabella, the more intellectual sister, corresponded with scholars throughout Italy. In 1493 a scholar in Cremona wrote her: "I hear that a man named Columbus lately discovered an island for the King of Spain." Thus did Isabella learn of the discovery of a New World by an Italian sailor from Genoa. But the voyages of Italy's native son would have a disastrous effect on Italian trade. The new discoveries would bring wealth to countries like Spain, Britain, France, and Holland.

The following year, 1494, the d'Este sisters' carefree existence came to an end. Charles VIII, the king of France, invaded Italy to claim the throne of Naples, which at one time had been ruled by a French noble. Unwisely, Ludovico Sforza allowed Charles to land his troops in a Milanese port. (Il Moro did so as part of his scheme to take the title of duke of Milan. His nephew, the duke, was related by marriage to the powerful king of Naples. If the king lost his throne, Il Moro could at last depose his nephew and take the title.)

However, Il Moro had set in motion a series of wars that would ultimately destroy him. It soon became clear that Charles VIII had designs on all of Italy, including Milan. The Italian states joined forces to force Charles out of the peninsula. Patriots spoke of the "war of Italy against her enemies."

Isabella's husband, Francesco Gonzaga, now the duke of Mantua, was chosen to lead the Italian army against Charles' forces. The two sides met near the town of Fornovo. The French had only 9,500 men, while the Italian forces numbered around 30,000. The Battle of Fornovo was fierce and bloody. At one point Francesco and a group of his men clashed with King Charles and his guards. Francesco spurred his horse forward and raised his sword to strike the king. But an arrow wounded the horse, and it reared up, throwing Francesco to the ground. The king escaped.

After the battle, 4,000 men lay dead, two-thirds of them Italian. Francesco declared he had won a victory, but in fact Fornovo was a major defeat. Historians call it the turning point in Italian history. Had the Italians destroyed Charles' army, they might well have remained politically united, strong enough to defend their independence. Instead, more invaders from the north followed. In the years to come, Italy would be divided up among the more powerful nations of Europe.

Furthermore, the gallant Francesco had sent a doctor to treat a wounded French officer. For this, he was suspected of disloyalty, and was relieved of his command. The disgrace embittered him and humiliated Isabella.

Ludovico did get the title of duke when his nephew died. But Beatrice, pregnant with their third child, learned that her husband had taken a mistress. This was not unusual for men of his rank, but Beatrice could not reconcile herself to it. She prayed constantly for God to change her husband's heart. Her maids feared that she was losing her mind. At a party on January 2, 1497, Beatrice tried to console herself by dancing. All night, she whirled around the hall in forced gaiety and then collapsed in exhaustion. She was taken to her room and died after midnight. She was only twenty-one.

Il Moro was shattered. He refused to see anyone for days and ate his meals while standing. He wrote a letter to the duke of Mantua, asking him to tell Isabella of her sister's death, for Il Moro himself could not bear to do it. Two years later a new French king, Louis XII, crossed the Alps and invaded Milan. Ludovico was captured and died in a French prison.

Isabella had urged her husband to come to the aid of Milan. Instead, he threw his support to the French, and when Louis XII captured Milan, Francesco joined the French king to celebrate the victory. Isabella never forgave her husband for the betrayal.

Still, she was realistic and proved to be a shrewd player in the complex game of Italian politics. She learned to manage the affairs of Mantua while her husband was fighting. When Francesco was taken prisoner in 1509, she ruled Mantua in his name. She told the commanders of her army not to surrender their forts even if her husband was brought to the gates and murdered before their eyes.

Her actions earned the respect of her subjects, but the cruel ingratitude of Francesco. When he was released, he wrote Isabella, "We are ashamed that it is our fate to have as wife a woman who is always ruled by her head." Isabella replied with spirit, "Your Excellency is indebted to me as never husband was to wife; nor must Your Excellency think that, even did you love and honor me more than any person in the world, you could repay my good faith."

From that time on, Isabella turned her back on her husband.

She lived only for two things: collecting fine objects, and advancing the careers of her sons. Isabella never had the wealth that her sister commanded, but she had excellent taste. Known as *la prima donna del Mondo*—the first lady of the world—she knew precisely what she wanted and would not tolerate delays. She oversaw the construction of a *studiolo*, or private study, for herself. She wrote the artist hired to decorate it:

> Since we have learned, by experience, that you are as slow in finishing your work as you are in everything else, we send this to remind you that for once you should change your nature, and that if our studiolo is not finished on our return, we intend to put you into the dungeon of the Castello. And this, we assure you, is no jest on our part.

She spent much time in the studiolo, where her personal art collection was displayed. It was a series of small rooms decorated with marble and inlaid wood panels. The panels showed outdoor scenes, musical instruments, and occult symbols. A door led to a secret garden, where Isabella admitted only her closest friends.

Isabella frequently ordered books from the Aldine Press in Venice, one of the new print-shops that opened after the new craft spread to Italy. The Aldine Press was famous for its beautiful typefaces—the printed letters. Some of them, including the style we call italic, are still in use today. But Isabella was a critical customer and would promptly send back books, if she did not like the paper they were printed on.

Though Isabella paid well, she demanded that artists create works exactly the way she wanted. One painter, Giovanni Bellini, irritatedly told her that "artists resent such strict directives, preferring to let their imagination roam." For years she pestered Leonardo da Vinci for "just a little picture," and even asked to examine the portrait da Vinci had painted of Ludovico Sforza's mistress. Among the long-suffering artists who worked for Isabella was Andrea Mantegna, who owned a Roman statue that Isabella particularly coveted. She continually offered to buy it, but he refused until, late in life, he badly needed money. Even then, she had her agent bargain the price down from what he wanted.

Isabella worked tirelessly to ensure that her three sons would hold positions of power and authority. When her husband died in 1519, her eldest son Federigo was only nineteen. At first, Isabella dominated him, keeping the reins of government in her hands. She arranged a suitable marriage for Federigo that would ensure a strong ally for Mantua. But Federigo had fallen in love with another woman, who encouraged him to resist his mother.

Isabella left Mantua for Rome, hoping to persuade the pope to name her second son, Ercole, as a cardinal of the Church. She spent two years in the effort. By now a new threat to Italy had appeared—the armies of the Holy Roman Emperor, Charles V. Back in Mantua, Federigo allowed them to pass through his territory without resistance; in return they spared his city. Charles' forces marched toward Rome.

Federigo wrote his mother, warning her to leave Rome. But she refused, for the pope had not yet granted her request. Thousands of others fled, fearing the worst. Finally, a few days before the enemy reached Rome, the pope awarded the red cardinal's hat to her son Ercole. Still Isabella did not leave.

On May 6, 1527, the army swept into Rome. The soldiers ran wild through the streets, grabbing up the treasures of the ancient city and slaughtering anyone who stood in their way. The screams of hapless people echoed through the city, and Isabella gave shelter to noblewomen, ambassadors and their families, priests, and friars. She boarded up the doors and windows and survived the dreadful sack of Rome.

On her return to Mantua, she was greeted as a heroine. People rushed forward to kiss her hand and touch her cloak. The war dragged on, and now a disease called plague swept through Italy. Mantua was not spared, and Isabella pawned her jewels to obtain money to relieve the misery of the sick and dying. Her prestige was now so great that Federigo had to give in at last and marry the woman his mother had chosen for him.

Isabella lived on into her sixties and continued to support the great artistic tradition of the era in which she lived. Titian, the great Venetian artist, painted two portraits of Isabella. One shows her as she was then; the other, as he imagined what she looked like as a young woman, when she was first married to the duke of Mantua. In both pictures, her dark eyes look out from the canvas, bright with the intelligence that made her one of the greatest figures of the Renaissance. Before she died in 1539, she told her eldest son, "I am a woman, and I learned to live in a man's world."

C H A P T E R 6

UNIVERSAL GENIUSES—
LEONARDO DA VINCI AND
MICHELANGELO BUONARROTI

In the year 1504, Florence was agog with excitement. Italy's two greatest artists had come to decorate the walls of the Palazzo della Signoria, where Florence's leaders met. Even to Florentines—who quite rightly regarded their city as the capital of Renaissance art—the chance to see Leonardo da Vinci and Michelangelo Buonarroti working on the same project was a special event.

Though it was not really a contest, people thought of it that way. At the time of the dramatic challenge, Leonardo was fifty-two. Michelangelo was not yet thirty, but was already thought of as a rival of the older man as the greatest artist in all Italy.

Ordinarily, younger artists were respectful to their elders, but Michelangelo did not hide his dislike for Leonardo. The reason is not completely clear. It may have been personal jealousy, for Leonardo, even in middle age, was known for his remarkably good looks and charming personality. Michelangelo, on the other hand, was painfully shy, and a broken nose had twisted his features. Furthermore, Leonardo slyly needled Michelangelo by remarking that painting (Leonardo's specialty) was more demanding than sculpture, the art in which Michelangelo excelled.

The Florentines took sides, arguing over the merits of each artist. Some called it the clash of the titans—and titans they were. Leonardo's many-sided genius in arts and sciences marks him as one of the most brilliant people who ever lived. Michelangelo's masterpieces, in both paint and sculpture, set a standard that has never been equaled. Even in Florence, where more geniuses lived in a single century than in any other place before or since, these two towered above the rest.

Unhappily for the world, the murals were never completed. Leonardo experimented with new paints, which changed color and ran down the wall. Leonardo shrugged and wandered off to pursue his many other interests. Michelangelo, whose services were always in demand, received a summons from the pope to come to Rome at once. He packed his paints and left his mural unfinished too.

We can judge these lost works only by reading the autobiography that another great Florentine artist, Benvenuto Cellini, wrote more than half a century later. As a wide-eyed boy of six, Cellini had watched the two artists working. He recalled that the partially finished murals remained on the wall for some time. "So long as they remained intact," he said, "they were the school of the world."

Leonardo's search for the mysteries of nature and life began in the little town of Vinci in the hills of Tuscany in 1452. His father, Piero da Vinci, was a lawyer who did not marry the barmaid named Caterina who bore his son. Yet Piero took the boy into his home and raised him. It soon became clear that Leonardo had unusual talents. He used chalk to sketch scenes from nature and made little models from clay. His father took some of them to the workshop of Andrea del Verocchio in Florence. Verocchio, already a famous artist, accepted the boy as an apprentice.

Workshops like Verocchio's turned out art of all kinds for anyone who would pay for it. A young apprentice soon learned how to make statues, jewelry, paintings, sets for theaters, and any other artistic products that customers wanted. Leonardo watched Verocchio and his assistants and soon was allowed to fill in small details of their work.

Watching was perhaps the greatest talent of the remarkable Leonardo. He developed the habit of taking a pad of paper with him whenever he walked through the city. He rapidly sketched faces in the crowd that struck him as especially beautiful or ugly. The country boy kept his love of nature and wild creatures. Sometimes, Leonardo bought some of the caged birds that shopkeepers displayed. He set them free.

Even in Florence, a city filled with people of talent and beauty, this young man stood out in a crowd. "Men saw this [gift of God] in Leonardo da Vinci," wrote the Renaissance art historian Giorgio Vasari, "whose personal beauty could not be exaggerated, whose

every movement was grace itself and whose abilities were so extraordinary that he could readily solve every difficulty." Vasari said Leonardo was so strong he could bend a horseshoe with one hand.

As Leonardo's skill increased, Verocchio let him do more important work. The workshop was hired to do a painting titled *The Baptism of Christ*. Verocchio assigned Leonardo to paint an angel standing near the main figures. But his angel was so superior to the rest of the painting (which still exists), that Verocchio realized his young apprentice had already surpassed him. By the time Leonardo was twenty, he had struck out on his own.

Watching and listening, Leonardo learned more than art in Florence. He loved to talk, and sought out people with knowledge of all kinds. The name "Renaissance man" still means anyone who is talented in many fields. Paolo Toscanelli was a Florentine scholar of mathematics, astronomy, geography, and medicine. From reading the accounts of travelers, he thought that China could be reached by sailing west across the Atlantic. In 1474, he sent a letter to another Italian, Christopher Columbus, encouraging him to attempt the voyage. As you know, Columbus followed the advice eighteen years later.

Another Florentine, Benedetto dell' Abacco, was interested in devising new inventions. He may have turned Leonardo to his life-long fascination with the way things work. The thousands of pages of Leonardo's notebooks are covered with designs for inventions that no one had ever thought of before. Even in those times, however, people were burned at the stake for having ideas that were thought to be too much like witchcraft. Perhaps that was why Leonardo used a code for writing in his notebooks. Left-handed, he wrote backward across the page in a reverse script that could only be read—by others—in a mirror.

Around 1482, when Leonardo was thirty, he applied for a position at the court of Ludovico Sforza in Milan. In his letter of application he listed the many things he could make—a light portable bridge for armies to cross rivers, pumps to empty the moat of a besieged castle, and even a spring-powered armored car.

Sforza, however, found Leonardo's artistic talents more useful. He asked Leonardo to make costumes and decorations for the parties his wife Beatrice gave. The artist was also a talented musician; he played a silver lute that he had made in the shape of a horse's skull. He also invented a heating and plumbing system for the palace.

In 1495 Leonardo started work on one of his masterpieces, *The Last Supper*, showing the last meal of Jesus and his disciples before his crucifixion. Ludovico had requested him to paint it as a fresco on a wall in a local monastery. But frescoes had to be painted quickly on fresh plaster before it dried. Leonardo thought that would allow too little time for his inspiration to strike, so he experimented with a new kind of paint for the project. A boy who watched Leonardo at work described him:

> He would often come to the convent at early dawn....Hastily mounting the scaffolding, he worked diligently till the shades of evening compelled him to cease, never thinking of food at all, so absorbed was he in his work. At other times he would remain there for three or four days without touching his picture, only coming for a few hours to remain before it, with folded arms, gazing at his figures as if to criticize himself.

Leonardo sketched people in the streets of Milan as models for the faces in the painting, with two exceptions—Jesus and Judas, the betrayer. Leonardo created the face of Christ from his own imagination. Judas was more difficult, and Leonardo haunted the neighborhoods where criminals lurked, searching for the most evil face he could find. The slow progress he made on the painting annoyed the prior of the monastery, who complained to Ludovico about Leonardo's "laziness." Leonardo responded by threatening to use the prior's face for Judas. That stopped the complaints. Alas, the paints that Leonardo used cracked and faded, so that what is left today is just a pale replica of the original masterpiece.

After the French invaded Milan in 1499 and took Ludovico prisoner, Leonardo looked for a new patron. For a time he returned to Florence, where he earned some money by painting a portrait of a merchant's wife. It is now the world's most famous painting—the *Mona Lisa*. All Leonardo's skills went into this masterpiece. He had always been interested in things others took for granted—the colors of shadows and air. The hazy landscape in the background of the *Mona Lisa* gives the picture some of its mysterious quality. The woman's face, with its haunting smile, has fascinated viewers through the ages.

Wherever he went, Leonardo added to his notebook entries on nature and science. He made endless sketches of birds, trying to discover the secret of flight. He drew plans for fantastic flying machines. One looks very much like a helicopter. He designed machines to manufacture cloth, similar to those actually used centuries later.

Artists of the time carefully studied the muscles of the human body to make their works as lifelike as possible. Leonardo secretly obtained dead bodies to cut apart, something that the Church frowned on. He drew cross sections of legs, arms, and skulls, as accurate as the drawings in a modern biology textbook. He showed that the body was a kind of machine: the muscles were levers, the eye a lens, and the heart a pump. Leonardo's life was a quest to find the secrets of just how nature works.

In Rome Pope Leo X commissioned Leonardo to do a small painting. But as usual Leonardo became distracted by technical matters. He devised a special varnish to preserve the picture—before he had even painted it. The pope threw up his hands in disgust, saying, "This man will never accomplish anything! He thinks of the end before the beginning." And Leonardo did not finish the project.

While in Rome, however, he did his only self-portrait. In red chalk, it shows a bearded old man with a huge wrinkled forehead and sad but piercing eyes. "O Time, thou that consumest all things!" he wrote in his notebook. Leonardo spent his last years in France, where he died in 1519. The most versatile genius who ever lived, he probably was lonely for someone who could share his fantastic vision of the world. Today, nearly five centuries after his death, science is still catching up with Leonardo da Vinci's ideas.

By the time Leonardo died, Michelangelo's fame as an artist had spread throughout Europe. Born in 1475, Michelangelo was the son of a minor Florentine nobleman. After his mother died when he was six, he was placed in the care of stonecutters. As a result, he learned to handle a hammer and chisel before he could read. His father took him back to Florence, where Michelangelo first entered school at the age of ten. He did not like it and spent much time with a friend who worked at an art studio. When his father learned about this he beat his son. But Michelangelo could be stubborn, particularly when art was involved. Finally Lodovico Buonarroti relinquished and apprenticed his son to an artist.

After only a year, the talent of the fourteen-year-old boy came to the attention of the ruler of Florence, Lorenzo de' Medici. Known as "the Magnificent," Lorenzo was a warm and generous man and a patron of the arts. He had decided to start a school in the garden of his palace to train promising youths as sculptors. Watching Michelangelo skillfully bring a stone faun to life with his chisel, Lorenzo was delighted. He took the boy into his household and treated him as an honored member of his family. Here, Michelangelo enjoyed the stimulating conversation of Florence's great philosophers and poets. This happy period lasted just three years. When Lorenzo died in 1492, the peace and security of Florence were shattered.

Michelangelo took his talents to Rome. He was twenty-one when he first saw the city that his genius would adorn with masterworks. Two years later, a French cardinal gave him a contract to produce a *Pietà*, or statue of the Virgin Mary with the dead Christ in her arms. The contract guaranteed that the statue "shall be the finest work in marble which Rome today can show." This was a confident pledge for a sculptor so young.

From the cold slab of marble, Michelangelo made the figures of Mary and Jesus come to life. The Virgin, in contrast to tradition, is shown as serene rather than grief-stricken. "If life pleases us," Michelangelo later wrote, "death, being made by the hands of the same creator, should not displease us." In no other sculpture are physical and spiritual beauty so perfectly united. When it was unveiled, all Rome marveled at it. Hearing someone say that another artist had made it, Michelangelo sneaked into the church at night and engraved his name on the base.

Michelangelo now had his pick of new projects. In 1501 he returned to Florence, the city he called his "nest." During his absence the Medici rulers had been driven out, but Michelangelo wanted to fulfill a dream that had begun in Lorenzo's household. Years before, he had seen a slab of marble called the "Giant." The eighteen-foot-high piece of fine Carrara marble had proved too difficult for earlier sculptors to work on. Florence's new rulers wanted someone to turn it into a work that would glorify the city. Michelangelo proposed a statue of the Biblical hero David and was awarded the project.

Working in a shed that had been built to enclose the huge slab, he left little time for food and sleep. Michelangelo's friend and biographer Vasari wrote that he ate only because it was necessary to live, usually chewing on a piece of bread as he worked. As for sleep, it

> rarely suits his constitution, since he continually suffers from pains in the head during slumber, and any excessive amount of sleep deranges his stomach. While he was in full vigor, he generally went to bed with his clothes on, even to the tall boots....At certain seasons he kept these boots on for such a length of time, that when he drew them off the skin came away together with the leather, like that of a sloughing snake.

Michelangelo's *David* was unveiled on September 8, 1504. A committee of artists, including Leonardo, decided to place it in front of the Palazzo della Signoria as guardian of the city. Ever since, it has represented an idea of physical perfection that the ancient Greeks had first admired. The Renaissance had begun with the rediscovery of the ideas of those Greek thinkers. Now an Italian had equaled, if not surpassed, the achievements of the classical world.

During the painting contest with Leonardo, Michelangelo received the message that took him again to Rome. There he met a man who would torment and goad him into creating yet another masterpiece—in paint, not marble. Pope Julius II recruited Michelangelo as part of a team of artists to beautify the city and glorify the papacy. Julius was as headstrong and proud as Michelangelo himself. Known as the warrior pope, Julius personally led troops into battle. He loved his military role. When Michelangelo was working on a huge statue of the pope, he asked Julius if he wanted to be shown holding a book. The pope replied: "What book? A sword! I know nothing about letters, not I."

Julius first demanded an immense tomb for himself. When Michelangelo showed the pope his plan, Julius was delighted and told the artist to proceed. Michelangelo traveled to Cararra, the best marble quarry in Italy, to select the finest stones.

But when he returned to Rome eight months later, Pope Julius was busy with another project—building a new cathedral of St. Peter. When Michelangelo asked to see the pope, he was kept waiting. Furthermore, Michelangelo had not been paid for work he had

already done. Insulted, he wrote an angry letter to the pope and fled to Florence. When the pope sent a messenger to bring him back, Michelangelo wrote, "If His Holiness now wishes to proceed, let him deposit the said money here in Florence."

After their quarrel had been settled, the erratic Pope Julius had new plans. He asked Michelangelo to paint the ceiling of the Sistine Chapel, where the pope said Mass. Michelangelo at first refused. "The place is wrong," he said, "and no painter I." But this time Julius got his way. In January 1509 Michelangelo climbed onto a scaffold and started to work.

For almost four years, the thirty-three-year-old artist filled the 130-foot-long ceiling with God's creation and the beginnings of human life on earth. Each day Michelangelo had to curl up on the scaffold, his face so close to the ceiling that the paint dribbled down into his beard. Eventually, he could not read letters or books except by holding them above his head. He asked his father to pray for him. "I strain more than any man who ever lived," he wrote a friend.

He also had to put up with Julius, who constantly appeared to urge him to hurry up. Once Julius went too far. He climbed the scaffold and struck the artist with his fists. Michelangelo immediately left Rome. But a papal messenger overtook him and not only apologized, but gave Michelangelo extra money. So the artist returned to his work—but when Julius again showed up to examine the progress, Michelangelo dropped a board to warn him to come no closer.

On October 31, 1512, the masterwork was unveiled. "All the world hastened from every part to view it," wrote Vasari, "and they remained amazed and speechless." Future viewers have felt no differently. In our own time, a complete restoration of the great work has shown how startling and bright the colors were when Michelangelo first put them on the ceiling.

Michelangelo would continue to create for many more years before he died at the age of ninety. As a true Renaissance man, he worked for fame and glory, but he also strove for absolute perfection and sometimes was not satisfied with the results. All his life he suffered from moods of intense despair. Vasari wrote: "His imagination was so perfect that he could not realize with his hands his great and sublime conceptions, and so frequently abandoned his works and [deliberately] spoiled many."

Years later another Pope, Paul III, flattered Michelangelo into returning to the Sistine Chapel. A new painting was needed for the wall. As Michelangelo had depicted the beginning of the world on the ceiling, now he would show the end—*The Last Judgment*. Michelangelo put his own portrait on the face of a saint whose skin had been stripped off and placed at the feet of Christ. Other faces on the wall were recognizable to Romans of the time.

One of the pope's assistants complained about the many nude figures, saying that the painting was "fit for a brothel or a tavern." In revenge, Michelangelo painted his critic among those condemned to Hell. When the man protested to the pope, Paul replied that he could pray a person out of Purgatory, but not out of Hell. But a later pope decided that the nudes were too distracting for a chapel dedicated to holy purposes. An artist was hired to paint cloths over the offending parts of nude figures. This artist earned himself the nickname of "Pants-maker."

As Michelangelo grew older, his work showed a deeper pessimism, and his style changed. Many of his later stone figures look almost unfinished—as if they were struggling to climb out of the stone itself. Yet they still inspire awe and wonder. Through the centuries Michelangelo has remained the standard of perfection in western art. Yet the *Pietà* was the only work he ever signed—that was the one that met his own standards.

CHAPTER 7

THE STARRY MESSENGER— GALILEO GALILEI

On January 7, 1610, a middle-aged professor of mathematics at the University of Padua eagerly waited for the sun to set. As darkness fell and the stars came out, Galileo Galilei climbed onto the roof of his house. The square, solid, red-haired man carried a long instrument that he called an "eye-reed." We would call it a telescope. Ever since he finished making his eye-reed, Galileo had gazed at the heavens whenever the weather was clear. Tonight he trained his lens on the planet Jupiter. To Galileo's amazement, he saw not only the planet, but also three other bright discs that changed position as he watched. A week later, he discovered a fourth.

Galileo eagerly discussed his discoveries with his colleagues. He wrote letters to other scientists in Italy. Soon he published a magnificent book, *Siderius Nuncius* (The Starry Messenger), which contained his description and drawings of his discoveries. He claimed to have seen

> stars in myriads, which have never been seen before, and which surpass the old, previously known, stars in number more than ten times.
> But that which will excite the greatest astonishment by far, and which indeed especially moved me to call the attention of all astronomers and philosophers, is this, namely that I have discovered four planets, neither known nor observed by any one of the astronomers before my time.

No human being had ever before seen the objects that Galileo described. They were in fact not planets, but the four largest moons of Jupiter. Although Jupiter and the other planets closest to the earth could be viewed with the naked eye, a telescope is needed to see smaller objects.

Galileo also trained his eye-reed on the earth's own moon and made another startling discovery. The moon did not have the smooth surface that people believed it did. "It is a most delightful sight to behold the body of the moon," Galileo wrote, "[It] certainly does not possess a smooth and polished surface, but one rough and uneven, and, just like the face of the earth itself, is everywhere full of vast protuberances, deep chasms, and sinuosities."

The news caused a sensation throughout Europe and Galileo's fame grew. He was the greatest scientist of his time, making discoveries in many branches of science. For his observations of the heavens, he deserves the honor of first astronaut. But Galileo's work earned him more than fame and honor. It also brought the condemnation of the Roman Catholic Church and very nearly cost Galileo his life.

Galileo Galilei was born in 1564, the year of Michelangelo's death. His birthplace was Pisa, site of the famous Leaning Tower, which could be seen from the noisy home of the Galilei family. Galileo's mother was a quarrelsome woman who, although she doted on her son, often made his life difficult. His father, Vincenzo, was a cloth merchant from Florence who came to Pisa to try to improve his business.

Vincenzo was a man of many talents. He was a fine mathematician and musician. While in Florence, he had been part of a group called the Camerata that had worked to develop a new type of music. Striving to combine music and words in a dramatic fashion, the members of the Camerata wrote some of the earliest operas—a musical form in which Italians would excel.

Young Galileo inherited his father's intellectual gifts. At an early age he could play the organ and the lute. As a boy, he made mechanical toys for himself and friends. When Galileo was about ten, his family returned to Florence where his formal schooling began. Even at this young age, Galileo was a skeptic. The usual method of teaching was for students to listen to and memorize everything the teachers said. But Galileo refused to believe something just because the teacher said it was so. His continual questioning irritated his teachers, but Galileo never allowed himself to be swayed by authority.

Galileo's ability was so great that his father sent him to the

medical school of the University of Pisa. Here Galileo became bored. Like almost all other subjects, medicine was taught from the theories of classical writers. The students were obliged to learn by heart the writings of Galen, a Greek doctor who had lived 1,400 years earlier, and Aristotle, an ancient Greek philosopher. Galileo thought he could learn more by observation and testing.

One day he was kneeling in the cathedral of Pisa, where a large lamp hung by a chain from the ceiling. Using a pole, an altar boy pulled the lamp to one side to light it. When the lamp was released, it swung back and forth in an arc. Galileo watched in fascination. Though the distance that the lamp traveled grew shorter, Galileo felt that each swing of the dwindling arc took the same amount of time. He had no watch, but he timed the swings against his own pulse beat. Finding that he was correct, Galileo experimented with his own pendulums and invented a machine that doctors could use to measure precisely their patients' heartbeats.

But his teachers were not impressed, and soon Galileo shifted to the mathematics department, where he felt more at home. Still a young man, Galileo was appointed professor of mathematics at the University of Pisa. Although the post did not pay well, it allowed Galileo time to work on his own ideas.

He shocked his fellow professors by declaring that one of Aristotle's basic ideas was wrong: that heavy objects fell at a faster speed than lighter ones. Galileo gathered a group of professors at the base of the Leaning Tower of Pisa. From the top, he dropped two objects of different weights. Both landed on the ground at the same time, proving that objects fall at the same rate despite their weight. Even so, the experiment changed few minds. So great was the authority of Aristotle that the teachers believed his books rather than the evidence of their own eyes.

Three years later, Galileo went to teach at the University of Padua. Padua was part of the Republic of Venice and prided itself on being a center of independent thought. Most Italian universities were closely linked to the Catholic Church. But Padua's students included not only Catholics but Protestants and Jews. Students and teachers were united in the quest for knowledge of all kinds.

In this atmosphere Galileo was a great success. Students came from all over Europe to hear him lecture. Because he was so short, a special raised stand had to be built so that the students could see him from the back of the room. Sometimes so many students showed up that he had to move his lectures outside.

Hearing that a Dutchman had made an instrument that made objects look larger, Galileo immediately set out to create one of his own. His first telescope could magnify up to ten times. He brought it to the Campanile, the bell tower that was the tallest building in Venice. The Doge, the ruler of Venice, and the city's senators huffed up the stairs to the top of the Campanile. They were astounded at what they saw. People walking in the streets below appeared close by. Distant ships far out to sea changed from tiny dots to full-sized vessels.

The Venetians, whose wealth depended on sea power, saw many practical uses for Galileo's telescope. Some of the senators were wealthy merchants who spent hours gazing out to sea, waiting for the return of their ships. A successful voyage meant great profits, but some ships were lost. Those merchants who learned in advance that a ship would return could make money buying shares in the voyage. Galileo's telescope cut two hours off the time it usually took to identify a ship far out at sea. The Senate gave Galileo a lifetime teaching job and doubled his salary.

Galileo turned his telescope to the heavens. As he explored the skies he became involved in a quarrel that split the scientific community. Galileo and his contemporaries believed in the theories of Ptolemy, a Greek who lived in Egypt in the second century A.D. In the Ptolomaic theory, the earth was the center of the universe. The sun and other planets revolved around it. In 1534 a scientist from Poland, Nicolaus Copernicus, had challenged this view. He claimed that the earth revolved about the sun. When Galileo studied the heavens with his telescope, he came to the conclusion that Copernicus was right.

The circumstances of the times demanded that Galileo act with extreme care. The Roman Catholic Church had denounced Copernicus' theories, and these were times when religious dissent was not taken lightly. In the past century a new form of Christianity—Protestantism—had challenged the authority of the pope and the Roman Catholic Church.

Faced with such a threat, the Catholic Church responded harshly. It strengthened the power of the Holy Office, or Inquisition, to search out heretics—anyone suspected of disloyalty to the Church's teachings. Ideas became a battleground, and new ideas were especially feared. Books regarded as dangerous were placed on a list of works that Catholics were forbidden to read.

Galileo quietly assembled proof that Copernicus' ideas could be correct. In 1616, he made a trip to Rome, where he pleaded with Church authorities to allow further study of the Copernican theory. But he failed. That year, the Church issued a formal condemnation, banning the teaching of the theory in any form.

Galileo continued his work privately. He took heart when a new pope was elected in 1623. He was Maffeo Barberini, a Florentine who took the name Urban VIII. Urban was reputed to be an intellectual. As a younger man, he wrote poetry and once had addressed a sonnet to Galileo and his book on astronomy.

So Galileo returned to Rome in 1624 to tell the new pope about his observations of nature:

> I think that in discussions of physical problems we ought to begin not from the authority of scriptural passages, but from sense-experiences and necessary demonstrations. Nor is God any less excellently revealed in Nature's actions than in the sacred statements of the Bible.

Encouraged by the meeting, Galileo believed that he could safely write a book on the Copernican theory, as long as he did not state outright that it was correct. He set out to write a dialogue in which both the Ptolemaic and Copernican world views were presented. He hoped that an intelligent person would be able to draw

the conclusion that the Copernican view was the correct one. In 1632 his *Dialogue on the Great World Systems* came into print.

The work immediately met with a storm of protest. The printer was told to stop his presses and destroy the book. In 1633 Galileo was called to Rome to defend himself before the Inquisition. He was now an old man of almost seventy years, suffering from a weak heart. On April 12 Galileo was led into a room where the Inquisitors waited.

They asked Galileo about his book and beliefs, accusing him of trickery in obtaining permission to publish it. Galileo was allowed to present his arguments, but his fate was sealed. In a closed meeting, with the pope himself presiding, it was decided that Galileo must be humiliated. He would be shown the instruments of torture as a warning, and forced to publicly recant, or retract his beliefs.

Faced with torture, Galileo gave in. Kneeling before the tribunal, he read aloud a statement that had been written for him "I, Galileo Galilei, son of the late Vincenzo Galilei," he began. He swore to "abandon the false opinion that the sun is the center of the world and immovable." He promised that in the future he would in no way teach, or even speak of, such "errors and heresies."

According to some stories, when Galileo finished he muttered under his breath, "Nevertheless, it [the earth] moves."

For the rest of his life Galileo was carefully watched. He retired to a country villa outside Florence. The Church ordered him not to publish any more books nor discuss in any way the forbidden doctrine, even in the privacy of his own home. Spies noted the names of his visitors. Yet he did not give up. Secretly he wrote a new book, not on the heavens but on the laws of this earth—his discoveries in physics. Somehow he managed to have it smuggled to the Netherlands, where it was published.

His health deteriorated, and soon he became totally blind. This was a terrible blow for he no longer could do what he loved most—examine nature and test for its inner laws. He wrote a letter in 1638 that shows his feelings of despair and isolation. "In my confusion and uncertainty, my mind jumps from one object of nature to the next. I cannot put my restless mind at ease, no matter how hard I try. Sleep has become impossible for me." He died four years later, not knowing that his ideas for learning through experiment would become the basis of modern science.

CHAPTER 8

THE GREAT TRICKSTER— ALESSANDRO DI CAGLIOSTRO

One evening in 1789, a line of splendid carriages dropped off their passengers at the gate of the Villa Malta. Some of the richest and most powerful people in Rome had received invitations to join a secret society known as the Roman Lodge of the Egyptian Order. It was promised that they would witness a demonstration of amazing power. The head of the Order offered a rare opportunity to share his knowledge of magical potions that could prolong life and increase wealth.

Who could resist? Cardinals of the Catholic Church and ambassadors from European countries were among those ushered into a large room in the villa. Sitting on a high three-legged stool at the center of the room was a short, heavy, ugly man—the Count Alessandro di Cagliostro. Cagliostro's outward appearance was off-set by his charm and obvious confidence. As servants shut the doors of the room, he began to speak in an eerie voice:

> It is fitting that I reveal who I am, that I open up my past....I see the endless desert, the giant palms project their shadows on the sand, the Nile flows quietly, the Sphinxes, the obelisks, the columns rise majestically. Here are the wonderful walls, the temples rising in great numbers....

Cagliostro seemed to be in a trance that took him to the ancient Egyptian city of Memphis. Soon he changed course and was in Jerusalem, where he heard voices praising a prophet. "Who is he? He is the Christ. Ah, I see him, at the wedding feast of Cana, turning water into wine."

Abruptly, the count jumped up from his seat, startling his listeners. He shouted that he too could perform Jesus' miracle. He promised to "reveal to you the mysteries. Nothing is unknown to me, I know all, I am immortal." Then he switched into Latin: *Ego*

sum qui sum. ("I am who I am.") As his spellbound guests watched, he poured a few drops of magic liquid into a carafe of water. The water turned purple, and Cagliostro took a sip. He proclaimed the concoction to be the finest wine of the ancient Romans. He passed the carafe around the room, and those who tried it pronounced it excellent.

Next Cagliostro produced a vial of "elixir number one." Choosing some of the oldest men in the room, he offered it to them. As they drank, their cheeks reddened and their eyes brightened—signs that this was truly a potion of youth. For his final act Cagliostro promised to show how he could enlarge the size of jewels. He took a jeweled ring from the French ambassador and placed it in a crucible. Chanting magic words that he said were Egyptian and Hebrew, he poured powder and liquids into the crucible. When he withdrew the ring, the jewel in it was more than twice its original size. The ambassador delightedly exclaimed that it was a miracle.

Not everyone in the audience was so impressed. Cagliostro was soon arrested. The meeting of the Roman Lodge of the Egyptian Order was the final performance of an amazing career. For twenty years, Cagliostro had tricked and astonished both rich and poor all over Europe.

This self-proclaimed miracle-man was neither a count nor was his real name Cagliostro. He was born Giuseppe Balsamo in Palermo, Sicily, on June 2, 1743. His parents hoped that he would become a priest and sent him to a monastery for his early education. The religious order that inhabited the monastery was dedicated to healing the sick. No doubt young Giuseppe picked up some knowledge of medical lore there. But he was unhappy with the strict life of the monastery and soon ran away.

He learned to live by his wits in the streets of Palermo. This "school of hard knocks" gave him an education in the folklore of many cultures. Sicily had been the first foreign province of the Roman Empire. Earlier, colonists from Greece and Carthage had settled there too. Over the years Sicily had been conquered by many people, including Arabs, French, Normans, Austrians, and Spaniards. It was now ruled by a Spanish prince. From this rich mixture of traditions and cultures, Giuseppe culled his wide knowledge of superstitions and primitive magic practices.

Giuseppe became a skilled magician, in an age when most people were all too willing to believe in the power of the supernatural. He sold potions, predicted the future, cast out demons, and made amulets that were supposed to guard the wearer from harm. If a client wished harm or even death to his enemies, Giuseppe could provide spells and potions to turn the trick. Giuseppe's greatest talent, however, was his ability to copy documents and signatures. He became so skillful a forger that even the original writer could not tell the difference. By the time Giuseppe Balsamo was twenty-five, he decided to seek his fortune in the wider world.

After reaching Rome, he met Lorenza Feliciano, the daughter of a craftsman. She became his wife and partner. Lorenza shared her husband's desire for wealth and fame. Her great beauty made her irresistible to men. She helped the ugly Giuseppe gain entrance to the homes of wealthy people. The two tricksters then fleeced their gullible victims.

Things became too hot for them in Rome, and they turned up next in Spain. Because they had little money, they dressed as pilgrims traveling to a religious shrine and begged for alms to help them on the way. This ploy took them to Portugal, where they used all the money they had to buy topazes, pretty but inexpensive gems from Brazil. It was not difficult for Giuseppe to interest unwary people in purchasing these "diamonds" at a bargain price.

By 1771 the couple was in London. Giuseppe now gave himself the title of an Italian nobleman. When their money ran out, Lorenza tried a desperate ploy. She knelt in prayer in a Catholic church, weeping as if her heart would break. When a wealthy Catholic, Sir Edward Hales, approached her, she poured out a sad tale of the poverty she and her husband suffered. Sir Edward gallantly hired her husband to paint murals on the walls of his country house. The fact that Giuseppe was Italian made him seem likely to have artistic talent. However, the murals he produced were so hideous that they had to be covered with whitewash.

Giuseppe quickly left England, returning to Palermo. This was a mistake, because he was arrested on a charge of forgery and thrown in jail. After his release he made his way back to London. Now he began to pass himself off as the Count Alessandro di Cagliostro (the last name of an aunt who was his godmother). He and Lorenza—now calling herself Serafina—persuaded people that they could predict the winning numbers in state lotteries. With the money they earned from selling predictions, they lived in high style and began to buy and sell jewels. But, after an English noble accused Cagliostro of stealing his jewels, the "count and countess" beat a hasty retreat from Britain.

They wandered to Germany and then Russia, looking for new opportunities. Cagliostro took up the practice of healing people with his supposedly magic powers. Indeed, many people reported that he cured them of illnesses when ordinary doctors had failed. Adding to his reputation, he declared that he wished to help the poor. Paupers sent their children to the gates of his house in the morning, and he treated them with as much care as his wealthy patients.

Cagliostro soon moved on to the scene of his greatest riches and glory—Paris. He gained entry to French society by striking up a friendship with Cardinal Louis de Rohan. The cardinal, a greedy man, was convinced that Cagliostro could turn ordinary metal into gold. "This man," said the Cardinal, "will make me the richest man in Europe." The Cardinal was so impressed that he set a bust of his friend on the stairway of his country estate, and inscribed it, "the Divine Cagliostro."

In Paris Cagliostro established the first lodge of his Egyptian Order. Among the advantages of membership in the order was the opportunity to buy two special elixirs. The first (and less expensive) would stop the aging process at the first sip. The second was more amazing yet. It could reverse the process, making the user up to thirty years younger, depending on how much of it was consumed. Gullible Parisians rushed to buy the elixirs in great quantity.

Cagliostro presented himself as living proof of the secret formula's effectiveness. For he claimed to be thousands of years old, and to prove it, he said he could remember events from all periods of his long life. To admiring audiences he would describe witnessing the building of the pyramids of Egypt. He told of meeting many of the Roman emperors and gave messages he had received from Jesus Christ. He appeared to have met virtually everybody in history, becoming the greatest name dropper of all time.

One of his most popular performances was communicating directly with spirits of the dead. These seances became extremely popular among wealthy Parisians, who flocked to Cagliostro's house to speak with friends and relatives from beyond the grave.

Cagliostro's success with the upper class was particularly amazing because his personal appearance was ordinarily repulsive. Few Europeans took regular baths in those days, but Cagliostro was exceptionally dirty and did not hide his body odor with perfume, as the rich did. The only language he spoke well was his Sicilian dialect.

Even so, he could hold a crowd spellbound. One skeptical witness described Cagliostro at a seance:

> I only stole a look at him, and I still do not know what to make of him: that face, that headdress, the whole appearance of the man, impressed me in spite of myself. I waited for him to speak. He talked some gibberish, a mixture of Italian and French, and gabbled quotations in something which passed for Arabic, but which he did not trouble to translate.

The great German writer Goethe became so intrigued that he set out to track down the magician's origins. Goethe went to Palermo and found the Balsamo family, who were simple, honest people living in a spotlessly clean house. Cagliostro's mother asked Goethe to remind her son to return some money he owed her. His mother seemed bemused by his new-found fame. "We are told," she told Goethe, "that Giuseppe lives like a very rich man. What luck would be ours if he returned here and took care of us!"

Ironically, Cagliostro's quackery was never exposed in France. His downfall came about through his relationship to Cardinal Rohan. That gullible man was taken in by another trickster and became involved in a scandal that rocked the country. It concerned the theft of a very precious necklace that belonged to the queen of France. Cagliostro was arrested along with the cardinal because of their close association. He soon proved that he was not involved, but he was ordered to leave the country.

As a parting shot, Cagliostro predicted that France would experience a great revolution, that the Bastille, the Paris jail, would be destroyed, and that "a great Prince" would arrive "who would reform religion." The year Cagliostro left France was 1786. Three years later the French Revolution began, and the mobs in Paris stormed the Bastille to set free the prisoners.

Cagliostro and Serafina fled to Italy. His invitation to the Roman notables was his final attempt to recoup his fortune. But it was not fraud or trickery that brought him down. Instead, he was charged with heresy and disrespect for the Church and the Christian religion. The Inquisition ordered him thrown in jail. Serafina, terrified, testified against her husband to save her own neck. Originally, Cagliostro was condemned to death but the sentence was changed to life imprisonment. He was locked up in the castle of San Leo in the Papal States.

As a final gesture, Cagliostro wrote a full confession to the pope, the territory's ruler. He signed it "Giuseppe Balsamo, repentant sinner." But the pope had no sympathy and refused to release him. For the rest of his life, the great Cagliostro remained in a tiny cell. The villagers who lived across the moat could sometimes see him clinging to the bars of his window. He shouted to them that he was an innocent man being tortured by despots. He died of apoplexy in August 1795 and was denied burial in a church cemetery. The last irony of his life was that Napoleon, the "French prince" whose rise to power Cagliostro had predicted, had by then invaded the Papal States. The French troops were liberating the prisoners of the pope along the way. Cagliostro died just before they reached him.

C H A P T E R   9

VICTOR EMMANUEL RE D'ITALIA— GIUSEPPE VERDI

The crowd at La Scala, the beautiful opera house in Milan, buzzed with excitement on the evening of March 9, 1842. The advance word about *Nabucco*, the new opera by Giuseppe Verdi, said that it would be a smash hit. Rumors leaked out from singers, musicians, scenery painters, candlemen, and ballet dancers that this was a work not to be missed. When Verdi slipped into his traditional seat within the orchestra pit, a cellist whispered to him, "Maestro, I would give anything to be in your place this evening."

As the music flowed forth, the audience quickly became spellbound. *Nabucco* was set in Biblical times. It was the story of King Nebuchadnezzar (the title character), who held the Israelites in bondage in Babylon. The audience heard a stirring cry for freedom. When the Israelites sang of their love for their lost homeland, the listeners were reminded of their own plight. Milan was ruled by the Austrians. Italy was disunited and not free. At the end of the third act, the words of the chorus—*Va, pensiero*—struck home:

> Go, thought, on golden wings;
> Go, rest yourself on the slopes and hills,
> Where, soft and warm, murmur
> The sweet breezes of our native soil.

People began to weep at the line, *O mia patria si bella e perduta!* ("O my country so beautiful and lost!") Cheers erupted throughout the hall and the audience shouted "Encore!" demanding that the chorus be repeated. This was against police regulations, for the Austrian authorities in Milan feared that encores could lead to demonstrations against the Austrian officials sitting in the boxes of the theater. But the cheers and clapping continued, making it impossible for the conductor to continue the opera. Finally he shrugged and signaled the singers to repeat the chorus. This time

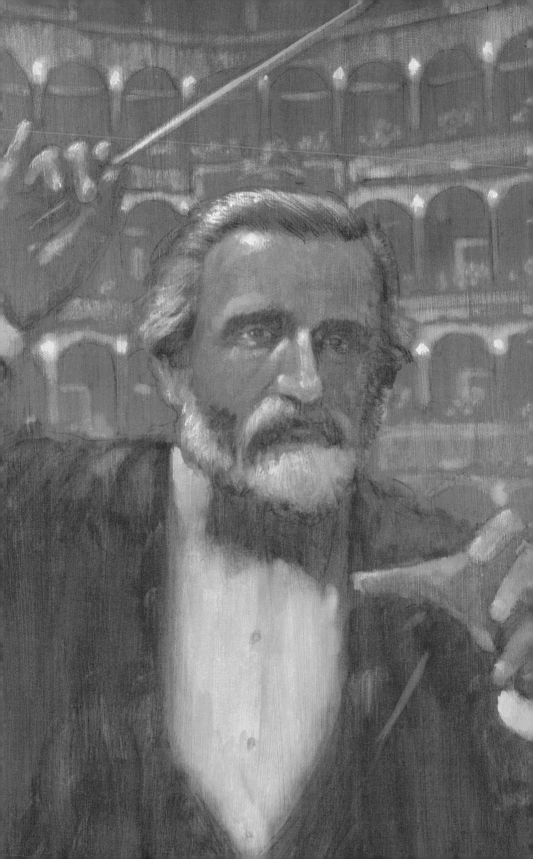

the entire audience defiantly joined in the singing.

Gaetano Donizetti, another great opera composer, was in the audience. His judgment on Verdi's new work was echoed throughout Milan: "Oh, that *Nabucco*. Beautiful, beautiful, beautiful." Many who attended the performance could not sleep that night. The next day the name Giuseppe Verdi was on everyone's lips. Almost immediately shopkeepers sold shawls alla Verdi, hats alla Verdi, and restaurants even offered sauces alla Verdi. Giuseppe Verdi had zoomed to the top in a land that adored opera.

The theme of his popular opera linked Verdi with the strongest emotion of the Italians of his time—their desire for unification and independence. In his lifetime, Italy would be a nation again after 1,500 years of disunity.

Verdi was born on October 10, 1813, in the tiny village of Le Roncole in Parma, in northern Italy. His father Carlo walked three miles to the larger town of Busseto to register his birth. The name entered was Joseph Fortunin François, for Parma was then part of the French Empire. In 1796, when Napoleon had invaded Italy, many Italian patriots had risen against their Austrian rulers to help him.

Napoleon's sympathy for Italy was not hard to understand. Born on the offshore island of Corsica, he grew up speaking Italian. Though Corsica was annexed by France only months before Napoleon's birth, his heritage and family were Italian. In a New Year's message in 1797, he spoke prophetic words: "Italy unfortunately has been long excluded from the number of the European powers....some day [the Italians] will see their country appear with glory among the powers of the earth." After ousting the Austrians Napoleon made Italy part of his French Empire.

Yet by the time of Verdi's birth, Parma was a battlefield. Napoleon was in retreat after his disastrous invasion of Russia. His enemies recaptured many of the areas he had conquered. Cossack troops looted Le Roncole in 1814. Luiga Verdi, with her infant son at her breast, climbed the bell tower of the church to escape the marauders.

Soon Napoleon was overthrown and in 1815, the Congress of Vienna met to redraw the map of Europe. The reactionary Austrian chancellor, Klemens von Metternich, had nothing but contempt for the nationalist ambitions of other people. "Italy," he remarked, "is merely a geographical expression."

The Italian peninsula was again divided into separate states. Austria directly ruled Lombardy and Venice (whose 1,000 years of independence ended with Napoleon's invasion). Relatives of the Austrian emperor controlled other states. Only the Papal States and the Kingdom of Piedmont-Sardinia were governed by Italians. But the brief years of freedom from Austrian rule had awakened the spirit of independence.

The Duchy of Parma, where young Giuseppe grew up, was ruled by Napoleon's former wife, Marie Louise, a member of the Austrian royal family. When the Austrian troops returned they carried out reprisals against those who had supported the French. As a youth, Verdi heard stories of the cruelty of the Austrians. Like other young people, he grew up with the flames of patriotism burning in his heart.

Verdi's family lived in modest circumstances. His father ran the village inn, barely eking out a living. But his son Giuseppe would remember the values of simplicity and hard work even after he was a world-famous celebrity. He maintained lifelong ties of affection to his parents. They sent him to the village school where he learned to play the organ. By the age of twelve he was the organist of Le Roncole's church. Realizing Giuseppe had exceptional talent, his father sent him to Busseto to continue his musical training.

At Busseto Giuseppe expanded his musical horizons, learning the craft of writing music. He studied for hours every day, taking a break only on Sundays when he walked to Le Roncole to perform his duties as the church organist. In Busseto he became friends with Antonio Barezzi, an older man who was a patron of music. Spending time in Barezzi's home, Verdi fell in love with his daughter, Margherita.

The town of Busseto seemed too small to hold Verdi's talents. Barezzi advised him to seek further training in Milan, the capital of Lombardy and the center of the Italian musical world. With a loan from Barezzi, Verdi went to take the test for applicants to the Milan conservatory of music. Usually, the conservatory took no students over fourteen—and Verdi was nineteen. Yet exceptions were made for students with extraordinary talent.

Verdi nervously awaited the results of his test. He was crushed when his application paper was returned. The conservatory had turned him down without giving any reason. The rejection was crushing. Verdi kept the paper, writing on it in his own words, *Fu respinta* ("Rejected.") Years later, when Verdi was the greatest name in Italian music, the conservatory asked to rename itself after him. Then it was Verdi's turn to reject the offer. "They wouldn't have me young; they can't have me old," he said.

Antonio Barezzi urged Verdi to stay in Milan since he had arranged to take private lessons with a talented teacher. A few years later, Verdi asked for Barezzi's permission to marry his daughter. The offer was accepted. The young couple took up residence in Milan and Verdi pursued his study of music.

In Italy opera was the queen of the arts. The combination of music and drama to form opera is one of Italy's many gifts to the world. Opera's popularity had spread ever since the sixteenth century, when humanists in Florence (including Galileo's father) began to recreate Greek musical dramas. Now, enthusiastic crowds flocked to opera performances throughout Italy. A nineteenth-century observer noted, "Every small town, every village has a theater. The poor may lack food, the rivers may lack bridges, the sick unprovided with hospitals…but we may be sure that the idle will not want a Coliseum of a kind."

The opera was a spectacle that stirred all the emotions from joy to sorrow. The Italians knew good singing and were a tough audience. Charles Dickens complained they seemed "always to be lying in wait for an opportunity to hiss." Some mean-spirited fans used candles to follow the libretto (book of the opera), watching for a mistake by the singers. If they noticed one, the cry would ring out from the darkness, *Brava, bestia*! ("Bravo, you beast!")

Gifted singers could become as famous as today's movie stars. Poems were written about them. *Prima donnas* ("First ladies") were showered with roses and handkerchiefs after a triumphal performance. But audiences also pelted singers they did not like with radishes and leeks—smelly vegetables.

Verdi was often tormented with doubt that he could succeed. His family had grown to include a daughter and a son, and he needed to earn money to support them. He completed the score for an opera called *Oberto* and was delighted when the director of La Scala accepted it. However, the lead singer fell ill during rehearsals, and the performance was canceled. One of the female singers, Giuseppina Strepponi, felt that the opera was too good to be shelved. She persuaded the director to reschedule it.

At the age of twenty-six, Verdi saw his first work performed in public. Audiences and critics liked it, and La Scala's director signed him up to write another one. But tragedy struck Verdi's personal life. Within three years, a series of illnesses took the lives of his daughter, his son, and finally his beloved wife. Despite his grief, he forced himself to write. But the first performance of the new opera was a fiasco. The audience hissed. Verdi vowed that he would never write another.

In his grief, Verdi withdrew into himself. He rarely left his home, earning a living by coaching singers. The director of La Scala knew that Verdi had too much talent to waste. So he offered Verdi a libretto that had been turned down by a famous composer. It was *Nabucco,* and Verdi set to work on the music for the opera that would bring him fame.

The success of *Nabucco* brought more offers. Giuseppina Strepponi took control of his career. Realizing how popular he was, she urged him to ask for an enormous amount of money for his next opera. Timidly, he did so and the producers agreed to pay it.

Verdi had touched a deep vein of patriotic feeling with *Nabucco.* Now he began to write operas on Italian historical themes, and the composer strengthened his ties with the Italian independence movement.

On a trip to London in 1847, Verdi visited the Italian patriot Giuseppe Mazzini. Mazzini had founded an organization called Young Italy to spread Italian patriotism throughout the peninsula. But the Austrian authorities drove him into exile.

Another patriot, Count Camille Cavour of the independent Kingdom of Piedmont-Sardinia, started a newspaper devoted to the Italian cause. The paper's name, *Il Risorgimento* (the resurrection), became the term for Italy's struggle for independence and unity.

In 1848 revolutions broke out all over Europe. In Milan and Venice, Italians attacked the Austrian troops. Verdi was thrilled at the news of the revolt. He planned a new opera to open in Rome the next year. It would celebrate the Battle of Leghorn in 1176, when the Italian cities defeated the forces of the Holy Roman Emperor. But Verdi's elated mood turned sour when he learned that the

Austrians had put down the rebellions in Lombardy.

Arriving in Rome, Verdi found the city celebrating the success of another patriotic action. Angered when the pope refused to support the Italians against the Austrians, Romans rioted and killed a papal secretary. The pope fled the city, and a republic was declared. Verdi's new opera, with its glorification of *la patria* (the nation), went on as scheduled—creating an uproarious success. During one performance a spectator became so overcome with emotion that he threw himself from the balcony.

The new Roman Republic was led by three triumvirs, a title taken from ancient Rome. One of them was Verdi's friend Mazzini. Romans took heart when the swashbuckling Giuseppe Garibaldi arrived with his band of red-shirted guerrilla soldiers. One of the militant members of Mazzini's Young Italy, Garibaldi had fled Italy thirteen years earlier under a death sentence. His subsequent career, fighting for freedom movements in South America, could form the plot of an opera. Now he was back to help his native land.

The pope called for help from other Catholic countries. France responded by sending troops to besiege Rome. Garibaldi did not have enough men to hold the city, but he saved his army by leading it north. Mazzini too escaped capture as the French captured Rome and returned the pope to his throne. Soon the revolts in the rest of Italy were put down as well.

Verdi was terribly depressed by the outcome. But in the 1850s he was in the prime of his artistic powers. He threw himself into his work with a vengeance, producing as many as three operas a year. From his pen came wonderful music that lights up opera houses all over the world today—including *Rigoletto*, *Il Trovatore*, and *La Traviata*. He bought a grand estate called the Villa Sant'Agatha outside Busseto, in his native Parma. He lived there with Giuseppina Strepponi, now as close to him as a wife.

He also formed a friendship with Count Cavour, who was by now the chief minister of the king of Piedmont-Sardinia, Victor Emmanuel II. Cavour took the lead in plotting the unification of Italy, with Victor Emmanuel as ruler. Secretly, Cavour signed an agreement with France, which called for that country to come to Piedmont's defense in case of war. At the same time, Cavour called for volunteers throughout Italy to join Piedmont's army.

When Austria demanded that Piedmont stop arming, Cavour

refused, and war broke out. With French help, the Piedmontese defeated the hated Austrians. More revolts began to break out throughout northern Italy, driving the foreign rulers out. Verdi himself led a delegation of citizens from Parma to unite their region with the growing Piedmontese kingdom.

The next step toward Italian unification was in the south. Patriots in Sicily were agitating for independence. They plastered the walls of Palermo with the graffiti, VIVA VERDI. To the foreign rulers, the slogan appeared to be enthusiasm for the famous composer. But it was really a secret message, to be read as an acronym—[V]ictor[E]mmanuel [R]e [d]'[I]talia, or "Victor Emmanuel, King of Italy."

Garibaldi landed on the island of Sicily with his Redshirts, a group of fearless men known as "The Thousand." All over the island, people rose up to join the fight. Soon Garibaldi was in control, and then launched an invasion of the mainland at Naples. There, too, Italians swarmed to his banner of freedom, and Garibaldi swept on toward Rome.

Troops from Piedmont-Sardinia moved south to link up with Garibaldi. They took much of the Papal States but spared Rome to avoid another conflict with France. In 1861 the new Kingdom of Italy was proclaimed, with Victor Emmanuel II as its king. The only parts of Italy not under his control were Rome, ruled by the pope, and Venice, still controlled by the Austrians.

When a new parliament was formed, Count Cavour asked Verdi to run as representative from Busseto. Verdi protested that he was not a politician, but Cavour told him that the country needed the prestige of his talents. Verdi won the election and entered the parliament at the new capital of Turin. He offered a plan to provide musical education to all children of the young country. This was a heady time, made even more joyful when Austria's defeat by Prussia in 1866 led to the inclusion of Venice in the new Italy.

In 1869 Verdi was offered a commission to write an opera for the new opera house in Cairo. The *khedive*, or ruler of Egypt, wanted only the best and was willing to pay a large sum. Verdi agreed. The result was *Aida*, the most popular opera ever written. Set in ancient Egypt, *Aida* is a tragic love story between a captured slave girl who was a king's daughter, and an Egyptian officer. The opera has everything—sublime arias, grand spectacle, and dance. It was to be performed in January 1871, but the scheduling was upset by international events. The costumes and sets were being created in Paris. Work was delayed by the outbreak of the Franco-Prussian War in 1870, which also caused the withdrawal of the French soldiers from Rome. Italian troops moved in, and Rome became the new capital of the Kingdom of Italy. The pope kept a small area around St. Peter's, known as Vatican City.

Verdi could now rest on his laurels. He had seen his dream of independence come true, and his many great works brought him respect and love not only in his homeland but from all opera lovers. Yet even as an old man, Verdi surprised his audience with new work. When Mazzini died, Verdi composed a great Requiem Mass for him. He also continued to produce major operas, including *Otello* and *Falstaff*, when he was in his seventies. He had married Strepponi in 1859, and they lived happily on their estate near the village of his birth. When Verdi died in Milan at the age of eighty-seven, the whole country mourned.

Verdi had requested a simple funeral with no music or singing. But as the crowd at the cemetery watched his coffin being lowered into the ground, they spontaneously took up the song *Va, pensiero*—"Go, thought, on golden wings." Italy's greatest opera composer could be best honored by the song that first brought him acclaim.

CHAPTER 10

LA DOTTORESSA—
MARIA MONTESSORI

At night the large room was gloomy, lit only by smoky oil lamps that hung from the ceiling. A strong smell pervaded the darkness, coming from several dead bodies that rested on stone slabs. The only living person there was a twenty-two-year-old woman, Maria Montessori. She was very tired, and ready to give up her dream.

Maria was the only female medical student at the University of Rome. It was not regarded as "proper" for her to dissect nude bodies in the presence of the male students. So she had to wait until classes were over and work during the night to complete her lab assignment.

Though Maria worked harder than anyone else, the male students jeered her in the halls. One of them liked to sit behind her in class and kick her chair to distract her from the lecture. Her father rarely spoke to her because he disapproved of Maria's foolish quest to become a doctor.

Why put up with all this? Maria thought. I can leave and become a teacher, as mother wants me to. She threw down her dissecting tools, put on her coat, and left the dissecting room. *Basta!* Enough!

As she walked through the streets, she felt like crying. She had worked so hard just to be admitted to the medical school. Yet everyone told her she was foolish. Perhaps she was.

Then she heard a voice. A woman dressed in rags held out her hand. She was begging for coins. Maria saw a small child, about two years old, playing on the ground next to the woman. There was a strange expression on the child's face. Despite its poverty and hunger, it was fascinated. The child had found a red strip of paper on the ground and was playing with it. Amazing—Maria thought—that such a simple thing could capture the child's interest and make her happy.

Something came over Maria, an emotion she later said she could not explain. There was work to be done. She had a chance to do something no other woman in Italy was allowed to do. Abruptly, she turned on her heel and went back to the dissecting room. She set to work. Never again would she let herself be discouraged.

Maria thought she was returning to the career she had chosen, as a doctor. But her life's work would in fact be known for something else—discovering the secret of that red piece of paper in the child's hands.

Maria Montessori was born in 1870 in the town of Chiaravalle, not far from the Adriatic coast in northern Italy. Her parents, Alessandro and Renilde, were ardent supporters of the unification of Italy. Alessandro, a soldier, proudly wore the medal he had earned in one of the battles for independence. He became a government official in the young country. His wife Renilde came from a family of scholars in Milan and had received an unusually good education for a woman. She passed on her respect for achievement and learning to her daughter. Maria's mother always suppported her ambitions, and the two remained close until Renilde's death in 1912.

The years of Maria's childhood were marked by the glow of Italy's pride in its newly won independence. Optimism about the country's future ran high, and Maria grew up feeling that Italians were on the verge of a new flowering of culture. She had the sense that she could accomplish great things.

Her parents raised her to have a strong sense of duty to her fellow human beings. From the time she was very young, she was expected to help the less fortunate. She knitted socks, shawls, and scarves for the poor—setting for herself a quota of knitting that she must complete each day. Although her family was well-off, Maria was expected to help with household chores.

When Maria was about five, the Montessori family moved to Rome, where she entered school. Maria was a good student and particularly liked arithmetic. She liked to be the leader in her games with other children and sometimes could be quite bossy. "Please remind me that I've made up my mind never to speak to you again," she would call out to playmates who annoyed her.

When she was thirteen, she surprised her parents by announcing that she planned to be an engineer. She then chose to go to the technical high school, instead of the classical high school that taught Greek and Latin. The technical school stressed mathematics, science, and modern languages. Almost all of its students were boys. The teachers did not know what to do with the few girl pupils at recess time, for they were "too old" to play with the boys. So the girls were shut up in a room by themselves.

After completing high school, Maria declared a new ambition. She wanted to be a doctor. Her stern father shook his head in disapproval. Such talk in 1890 was unheard of for an Italian woman. "What will I be when I grow up?" was not a pressing problem for most girls. They would be wives and mothers. Maria's own mother suggested that if she had to work, why not be a teacher? Teaching was just about the only career open to respectable women.

But Maria had her mind set on medicine. Although he disapproved, Alessandro agreed to take his daughter to see Guido Baccelli, the head of the medical faculty at the University of Rome. Alessandro believed that Professor Baccelli would support his opposition to Maria's plans. Baccelli listened politely as Maria presented her case for admission to the medical school. But he refused to encourage her. As they were leaving, Maria shook hands with Baccelli and vowed, "I know I shall become a doctor."

Maria persisted. She wrote letters to the university and sent recommendations from her teachers. Two years later her efforts bore fruit. She was accepted as the first woman medical student in Italy.

After her crisis of confidence in the laboratory, she silenced the taunts of the male students by laughing when they whistled at her in the halls. "The harder you blow the higher I'll go," she said. And her work paid off. She won a cash prize given each year to the student who did the best work on the study of disease. Later she competed with the other students for an assistantship in the hospital. The post was awarded to Maria.

Even her father came around. During the last year of medical school, each student was required to give a lecture to the class. Maria feared that her fellow students might jeer her performance.

Instead, they rose and applauded when she finished. Without telling Maria, her father had come to hear her lecture. Now, when he saw the praise that others showered on her, he admitted that he had been wrong.

Maria graduated near the top of her class as the first modern Italian woman doctor. A special diploma had to be made for her, for the ordinary ones used only male words like *Dottore*. Newspapers printed stories about this unusual event, and Maria became a celebrity. She was called *la giovane Dottoressa Montessori*—the young Doctor Montessori.

Now she was in demand to speak before groups working for the cause of women's rights. Speaking to a group of Roman women, she declared that "women can and should do more with their lives than what they are allowed to do today."

Maria decided to specialize in children's medicine. She worked in a hospital, but also visited her patients in their homes. Sometimes she would spend the whole day there, preparing food and caring for the children as if they were her own. Once she visited a woman who had just given birth to twins who were not expected to live. La Dottoressa put the mother to bed and carefully treated the sickly twins. They both survived, and years later their mother pointed out La Dottoressa in a Roman park and told them, "She is your mother. She gave you life."

Maria continued to study and soon became interested in mental disorders. She went to see some retarded children, a visit that began her study of children's education. At that time, retarded children were kept in insane asylums with adult men and women. When Maria first visited one of these ghastly places, she found that the room in which the children were kept was completely bare. The children huddled on benches, squatted on the floor, or wandered aimlessly with vacant eyes. Their attendant called them disgusting. When Maria asked why, the woman responded that they crawled around the floor like dogs to find crumbs left from their meals. They played with the crumbs like toys. Maria realized that the children had nothing else to play with. Their minds were active— showing that the children needed some stimulation.

The more Maria saw of these children, the more she wanted to find a way to help them. She went to the library to do research on treatments of retarded children in other countries. She began to create special toys to stimulate the children. She worked with them long hours each day. Her work brought success. People were amazed when some of the "retarded" children actually passed the regular school examinations!

This success made Maria decide to see if she could improve the education of normal children. She got a chance in 1907 when she was placed in charge of the Casa dei Bambini (the children's house) at the San Lorenzo housing project on the outskirts of Rome. The Casa was what we would call a day-care center for poor children. While their parents were at work, these children had roamed the buildings, scrawling on walls and getting into trouble. They were considered too uncontrollable for anyone to teach them anything.

But on the day the Casa opened, Maria claimed she "had a vision and, inspired by it, I was inflamed and said that this work we were undertaking would prove to be very important and that someday people would come from all over to see it."

Maria had developed what was then a revolutionary idea: small children taught themselves. The duty of the teacher was to provide the right surrroundings and equipment for them to work with. She believed that all children wanted to learn, and could, if they were treated with respect.

La Dottoressa ordered child-sized tables and chairs so the children would feel the room was for them alone. She began to make "toys" that the children could use to correct their own mistakes. For

example, her Pink Tower was a set of ten cubes that varied in size. By trying to stack them up, a child would see that the large ones had to go on the bottom. Through trial and error, the child would learn the sequence necessary to build the tower.

Maria provided color boxes and counting boxes, boards where tiny fingers could contrast rough and smooth surfaces, and pieces of cloth to let the children fit buttons into holes. One of the most popular Montessori materials was a set of small cylinders of different sizes that fit into corresponding holes in a wooden block.

Even Maria was amazed at the success of her work. Within six months she saw a tremendous change in the children. They waited at the door in the morning for the teachers to arrive. They almost never fought with each other and worked for hours on the materials she had made. When some wealthy Romans presented the Casa with regular toys, the children ignored them. They preferred Maria's learning tools.

La Dottoressa also stressed cleanliness and neatness. A small washbasin encouraged the children to wash their hands and clean up at the end of the day. Each "toy" had a special place on the shelves, and the children carefully put them back when they were finished.

Soon word spread of her success, and people came to observe. One of the visitors was Queen Margherita of Italy, who spent days watching the children. She was particularly intrigued by a little girl who had not even noticed when the queen arrived because she was so engrossed in her task. It reminded the queen of a story about Dante. He was sitting on a bench in Florence reading a book. A group of entertainers began to play and dance in front of him. Asked whether he enjoyed the performance, he was surprised. He had not heard or seen it because he was reading.

More Montessori Casas opened. Maria offered a course for teachers to learn her new method. Teachers came from all over Europe. In 1913 La Dottoressa traveled to the United States where she got a tremendous welcome. The inventors Alexander Graham Bell and Thomas Edison praised her system. Five thousand people came to hear La Dottoressa speak at New York's Carnegie Hall and many had to be turned away. President Woodrow Wilson's daughter became head of the Montessori Society in the United States.

When World War I broke out in 1914, Maria spread her doctrine to Spain, a neutral country. She was appalled at the suffering the war brought on, and she stayed in Spain till it was over. She became a spokesperson for peace, believing that people who were treated with respect as children were less likely to be warlike as adults.

After the war, Maria went to Great Britain and other countries to set up demonstration schools. Her emphasis on educating children for peace brought her into conflict with the new Italian government. In 1922, Benito Mussolini came to power by leading a group of his black-shirted supporters in a March on Rome. Mussolini was intoxicated with the idea of restoring Italy to the greatness of ancient Rome. He named his political party the Fascists, taking the name from the bundle of sticks (*fasces*) that had been a badge of office for Roman officials.

Mussolini ruled as a dictator—the title that the Roman Senate had sometimes given in times of crisis. He curtailed freedoms of speech and press and encouraged a military spirit in the young. At the age of four, boys became part of units called "Sons of the She-Wolf," named for the wolf that nursed Romulus and Remus. Although Mussolini at first tolerated the Montessori schools, they were shut down by the mid-1930s.

Maria fled her homeland and lived in Spain until a civil war broke out there. Mussolini and his ally Adolf Hitler soon brought on a war that engulfed Europe. Montessori went to India and stayed there during World War II. India fascinated her and though she was now seventy, she continued to teach others how to use her methods.

In the postwar years La Dottoressa was more famous than ever. Montessori Congresses brought together educators from all over the world. La Dottoressa worked with the United Nations to urge the world to solve the problems of hunger and ignorance. She had achieved a great deal during her lifetime, and her doctors urged her to slow down. But she continued to travel and speak, preparing for a trip to Africa on the day she died in 1952, at the age of eighty-two.

Maria blazed a trail that others followed. Educators now realize the importance of early childhood education. The Head Start program in the United States uses some of the philosophy and materials of La Dottoressa. Her life is one more example of an Italian enriching the world.

G L O S S A R Y

Augur: A person who interpreted the flight of birds to reach decisions.

Caput Mundi: "Head of the World," the title of Rome during the Empire.

Consul: One of the two elected leaders of the government of the Roman Republic.

Copernican theory: The scientific belief, put forth in 1534 by Nicolaus Copernicus, that the earth and the other planets revolved around the sun. See *Ptolemaic theory*.

Fasces: A bundle of rods enclosing an axe; used as a symbol of Roman power.

Fresco: A type of wall painting that has to be painted quickly on fresh plaster.

First Triumvirate: An alliance between Julius Caesar, Crassus, and Pompey.

Guild: A group of crafts workers united to increase their power.

Heretic: Anyone who believes or questions the teachings of an established church—in this book, the Catholic Church.

Holy Roman Emperor: A German prince who took the title passed down from Charlemagne.

Inquisition: Agency of the Roman Catholic Church that sought to find and punish heretics. Also called the Holy Office of the Inquisition.

Layman: A church member who is not a priest.

Legion: The basic unit of the Roman Army; in Julius Caesar's time, it had around 4,000 men.

Pax Romana: "Roman Peace," enforced throughout the empire for two hundred years after the first emperor's reign.

Pontifex Maximus: A Roman official who supervised all the sacred rituals in the city.

Prima Donna: "First Lady," a term applied to a woman who excels in anything from opera to patronage of arts.

Ptolemaic theory: The ancient scientific belief that the earth was the center of the universe, and that the sun, planets, and stars revolved around it.

Renaissance: The time of rebirth of interest in the classical learning and art of Greece and Rome, from around 1350 to 1550, when Italy's civilization rose to new heights.

Risorgimento: "Resurrection," the term used for Italy's nineteenth-century struggle for independence and unity.

Triumph: A public celebration of a Roman military victory.

Triumvir: One of three men who agreed to share power in ancient Rome.

Troubadour: A wandering poet who sang songs of love.

Vestal Virgin: One of the guardians of the sacred fire of Rome.

B I B L I O G R A P H Y

Bainton, Roland, H., *The Horizon History of Christianity*, New York: Avon Books, 1964.

Barrett, Kathrine, ed., *Italy*, Singapore: APA Publications, 1991.

Barzini, Luigi, *The Italians*, New York: Atheneum, 1965.

Bentley, James, *A Guide to Tuscany*, New York: Viking, 1987.

Bingham, Marjorie Wall, and Gross, Susan Hill, *Women in Ancient Greece and Rome*, St. Louis Park, MN: Glenhurst Publications, 1983.

Boorstin, Daniel J., *The Discoverers*, New York: Vintage Books, 1985.

Bronowski, Jacob, *The Ascent of Man*, Boston: Little Brown & Co., 1973.

Cartwright, Julia, *Isabella D'Este: A Study of the Renaissance*, New York: E.P. Dutton, 1907.

Cartwright, Julia, *Beatrice D'Este: Duchess of Milan*, New York: E.P. Dutton, 1926.

Casson, Lionel, ed., *Classical Age*, New York: Dell, 1965.

Coughlan, Robert, *The World of Michelangelo, 1475-1564*, New York: Time-Life Books, 1966.

Cronin, Vincent, *The Horizon Concise History of Italy*, New York: American Heritage Publishing Co., 1972.

Grant, Michael, *Myths of the Greeks and Romans*, New York: New American Library, 1962.

Hadas, Moses, *Imperial Rome*, New York: Time-Life Books, 1965.

Hauser, Ernest O., *Italy, a Cultural Guide*, New York: Atheneum, 1981.

Hibbert, Christopher, *Rome: The Biography of a City*, New York: Penguin Books, 1985.

Howell, A.G. Ferrers, *Dante: His Life and Work*, Port Washington, NY: Kennikat Press, 1969.

Hunt, Morton M., *The Natural History of Love*, New York: Knopf, 1959.

Kramer, Rita, *Maria Montessori*, New York: Putnam's, 1976.

Livy, *The Early History of Rome*, trans. Aubrey de Selincourt, Baltimore: Penguin Books, 1969.

Marek, George R., *The Bed and the Throne: The Life of Isabella d'Este*, New York: Harper & Row, 1976.

Martin, George, *Verdi: His Music, Life and Times*, New York: Dodd, Mead & Co., 1983.

Nicolson, Harold, *The Age of Reason (1700-1789)*, London: Panther Books, 1968.

Payne, Robert, *Ancient Rome*, New York: American Heritage Press, 1970.

Plumb, J.H., ed., *Renaissance Profiles*, New York: Harper Torchbooks, 1961.

Plutarch, *Makers of Rome*, trans. Ian Scott-Kilvert, New York: Penguin Books, 1965.

Suetonius, *The Twelve Caesars*, trans. Robert Graves, Hammondsworth, England: Penguin Books, 1969.

Toynbee, Paget, *Dante Alighieri: His Life and Works*, New York: Harper Torchbooks, 1965.

Wallace, Robert, *The World of Leonardo, 1452-1519*, New York: Time-Life Books, 1966.

S O U R C E S

Introduction: The City that Conquered the World

page 4: "I sing of arms…" Grant, Michael, Myths of the Greeks and
Romans, p. 285.

page 5: "So perish any other…" Livy, The Early History of Rome, p. 24.

Chapter 1: Julius Caesar

page 8: "Of all the honors voted him…" Suetonius, The Twelve Caesars,
p. 29.

page 10: "When I see his hair…" Hunt, Morton M., The Natural History of
Love, p. 68.

page 12: "Now that I am the leading Roman…" Suetonius, op. cit., p. 22.

page 14: "an instrument of wrath…" Payne, Robert, Ancient Rome, p. 141.

Chapter 2: Suetonius

page 16: "You are a thoughtless fool…" Casson, Lionel, ed., Classical Age,
p. 573.

page 16: "Shut up your house…" Ibid., p. 574.

page 18: "Such a throng…" Hadas, Moses, Imperial Rome, p. 45.

page 18: "Many are the opportunities…" Hibbert, Christopher, Rome: The
Biography of a City, p. 49.

page 20: "so strong that he could…" Suetonius, op. cit., p. 143.

page 20: "established a shrine to himself…" Ibid., p. 160.

page 21: "No matter where Claudius…" Ibid., p. 201.

page 21: "He tried to poison her three times…" Ibid., p. 227.

page 22: "No one was allowed to leave the theater…" Ibid., p. 238.

Chapter 3: St. Francis of Assisi

page 25: "From now on…" Hauser, Ernest O., Italy, p. 94.

page 26: "What's the matter…" Bainton, Roland H. The Horizon History of
Christianity, p. 201.

page 29: "Lord, I give you back this family…" Hauser, op. cit., p. 97.

page 30: "Praise to you, My Lord…" Ibid., p. 98.

Chapter 4: Dante

page 31: "a subdued and excellent crimson…" Bentley, James, A Guide to
Tuscany, p. 54.

page 33: "she turned her eyes…" Ibid., p. 54.

page 35: "I wonder," said the lord… Toynbee, Paget, Dante Alighieri: His
Life and Works, p. 145.

page 37: "Besides, what does it…" Holme, Timothy, Vile Florentines,
p. 115.

page 38: "See how his beard is frizzled…" Howell, A.G.
Ferrers, Dante: His Life and Work, p. 22.

Chapter 5: Isabella and Beatrice d'Este

page 43: "I…asked her questions…" Marek, George R., The Bed and the
Throne, p. 24.

page 44: "We went out hunting..." Ibid., p. 159.

page 44: "When I read your letter..." Ibid., p. 101.

page 45: "I hear that a man named Columbus..." Cartwright, Julia, Isabella D'Este: A Study of the Renaissance, p. 96.

page 46: "We are ashamed..." Plumb, J.H., Renaissance Profiles, p. 151.

page 47: "Since we have learned..." Cartwright, Julia, Isabella D'Este, pp. 88-89.

page 47: "Artists resent..." Hauser, op. cit., p. 87.

Chapter 6: Leonardo da Vinci and Michelangelo Buonarroti

page 50: "So long as they remained..." Coughlan, Robert, The World of Michelangelo, p. 95.

pages 51-52: "Men saw this [gift of God]..." Wallace, Robert, The World of Leonardo, p. 12.

page 53: "He would often come..." Ibid., p. 81.

page 54: "This man will never..." Ibid., p. 150.

page 55: "If life pleases us," Coughlan, op. cit., p. 76.

page 56: "rarely suits his constitution..." Ibid., p. 87.

page 57: "If His Holiness now wishes..." Plumb, op. cit., p. 48.

page 57: "I strain more..." Coughlan, op. cit., p. 114.

Chapter 7: Galileo Galilei

page 59: "stars in myriads..." Bronowski, Jacob, The Ascent of Man, p. 204.

page 60: "[It] certainly does not possess..." Ibid., p. 204.

page 64: "I think that in discussions..." Ibid., p. 209.

page 65: "I, Galileo Galilei..." Ibid., p. 216.

page 65: "In my confusion..." Boorstin, Daniel J., The Discoverers, p. 78.

Chapter 8: Alessandro di Cagliostro

page 66: "It is fitting..." Barzini, Luigi, The Italians, p. 97.

page 71: "I only stole a look..." Encyclopedia Britannica, 1969 ed., vol. 4, pp. 579-80.

pages 71-72: "We are told..." Barzini, op. cit., p. 94.

page 72: "Giuseppe Balsamo, repentant sinner," Nicolson, Harold, The Age of Reason, p. 413.

Chapter 9: Giuseppi Verdi

page 73: "Maestro, I would give anything..." Martin, George, Verdi: His Music, Life and Times, p. 102.

page 73: "Go thought..." Ibid., p. 103.

page 75: "Italy unfortunately has been..." Cronin, Vincent, The Horizon Concise History of Italy, p. 179.

page 77: "Every small town..." Barrett, Kathrine, ed., Italy, p. 300.

Chapter 10: Maria Montessori

page 86: "women can and should..." Kramer, Rita, Maria Montessori, p. 81.

page 87: "had a vision..." Ibid., p. 112.

INDEX